FOREWORD

I first met Chef John Schumacher, ironically enough, on a fishing trip for salmon on Lake Michigan. He was an instant charmer.

What I remember most was John's enthusiasm for life and for taking my dollar bet on the first fish.

Now, years later, my favorite chef still maintains his enthusiasm for life, for food and for fishing. His achievements in the kitchen or over a campfire are legendary.

Indeed, Chef John is the "Game Gourmet."

This is not an act. He baits his own hook. As an avid fisherman, Chef John has paid his dues on the other end of the line. He understands the joys of angling, the trials and tribulations of catching nothing and the spirit of sharing nature's world.

Plus, the guy can cook.

When my television show, Minnesota Bound, was still on the drawing board, we wanted to show audiences the full circle of life as an outdoor enthusiast. Obviously, this includes keeping and eating some of what you catch. Yes, we believe in catch and release, but it's also not a sin to enjoy a meal of fresh fish. A better way is to select the fish to release (usually the largest) and to keep (usually the smallest).

When Minnesota Bound premiered, Chef John was an immediate star with a fast-paced 2-minute lesson on how to make fish cooking easy and exceptionally tasty. And unique.

In fact, that's my favorite word for describing a day with Chef John in the kitchen or in a fishing boat. Unique. That he is.

Best regards,
Ron Schara, host
Minnesota Bound television show

D1567813

Dear Readers,

The recipes in this book have all been presented on the **Minnesota Bound** & **Backroads with Ron and Raven** television shows and in some of my other cookbooks and cooking videos.

They are my personal favorites that I take on camping, hunting and fishing trips.

These recipes were chosen because they are easy to prepare and the ingredients are basic and readily available.

Good Eatin'
Chef John Schumacher

FOOD HANDLING AND SAFETY TIPS FOR THE TRIP

1. Safe drinking water has over the years become more and more important. Never trust your taste, smell or sight or how far you are from civilization for safe drinking water. Water contamination comes from animal and human wastes.

2. Drink bottled water if possible. To be extra safe, drink carbonated water (especially in North America). Carbon dioxide brings the water acid to 4.2 which kills bacteria.

3. Bring water to a boil for longer than 5 minutes. To be extra safe, boil water 25 minutes at a slow rolling boil.

4. When using bleach to purify water, add 1 teaspoon per gallon and let set for at least 1 hour.

5. Make sure to use a name brand water purification kit.

6. To purify water using pure lemon juice or vinegar, use 1 cup per gallon. Let sit 1 hour.

7. If camping, make sure the outhouse is as far from camp as possible.

8. Wash your hands thoroughly with a brush.

9. Hold all cooked foods above 150° or keep them below 40°.

10. Do not poke potatoes or vegetables with a fork. This will contaminate the inside of the vegetable.

11. Never roast potatoes in foil. Potatoes are grown in dirt. That is a source of botulism.

12. When camping, use herbed salad dressing as a marinade to fuse flavors. It has vinegar in it which will bring the pH to 4.1.

13. There are 16 kinds of E Coli. You must cook all ground meat to at least 155° or higher which is medium well to well done.

14. Be careful of bird droppings. They are just as dangerous as rodent droppings.

15. Make sure all boxes, coolers and pails are clean on the bottom.

16. 1 out of every 20,000 egg yolks has salmonella. Make scrambled eggs well cooked.

17. Wash all fruits with stems with warm water not cold because cold water will cause vegetables to absorb bacteria into the stem end.

18. Be very careful of salad greens. Wash them well.

19. Quinine or tonic water is very safe to drink. That is why the English started drinking gin and tonics in Africa.

20. Never use sponges. They are a place for germs to grow.

21. When packing for camp, keep meats, dairy and vegetables in separate bags as they may contaminate each other.

22. Do not take doggy bags from restaurants.

23. Always clean all equipment and knives after cutting especially after cutting fowl or poultry. Wash with a vinegar or bleach solution. Soap only cuts grease. It does not kill germs unless it states on the label that it is anti-bacteria soap.

24. I suggest washing everything as close to cooking as possible. Cook as close to eating as possible. When camping, try not to have leftovers as refrigeration is limited.

25. For coolers, use sealed freezer packs or sealed containers of frozen ice as melted ice spreads germs.

26. Never eat yellow snow.

FISH RECIPES

1. Rhode Island Fish Chowder
2. Creamy Fish Chowder
3. Fish in a Tin Pouch
4. Easy Pan Fish Chips
5. Beer Battered Fish
6. Fish Tacos
7. Grilled Fish T-Bone Steaks with Anchovy Caper Butt
8. Grilled Salmon
9. Farmwife Fish Fillets
10. Italian Stuffed Fish
11. Fried Whole Pan Fish
12. Fish Chili
13. Fish in a Red Sea Bag
14. Fish Stir Fry
15. Poached Fillets with Cucumber Sauce
16. The Fish is in the Bag
17. Fish Casino
18. Fish BLT Triple Deckers
19. Gravlax

FISH SIDE DISH RECIPES

Fish Recipes

RHODE ISLAND FISH CHOWDER

In a heavy stock pot, render salt pork to light brown. Add onions, celery, carrots and garlic. Cook until onions are transparent. Stir with a wooden spoon to keep from burning. Add thyme, black pepper and clam broth. Simmer for 30 minutes. Add tomato soup and potatoes. Simmer until potatoes are tender for about 20 minutes. Add fish pieces and simmer 5 minutes. Remove from heat. Cover and let steep for 10 minutes. Adjust seasonings to taste and serve.

Chef John's Tips

- This is my favorite chowder.

- It is very important to use salt pork and Campbell's tomato soup. The flavors are just right. Try not to substitute these ingredients.

- If salt pork is not available, use diced bacon.

- If clam broth is not available, use fish stock or chicken stock.

Rhode Island Fish Chowder Ingredients

- 1 cup salt pork, diced 1/4"
- 2 cups onions, diced 1/4"
- 1 cup celery, diced 1/4"
- 1 cup carrots, diced 1/4"
- 2 cloves garlic, minced fine
- 1 Tbsp. fresh thyme
- 1/4 tsp. black pepper, freshly grated
- 1 quart clam broth
- 3 cans Campbell's tomato soup
- 3 cups red potatoes, skins on, cut into 1/2" cubes
- 4 cups boneless fish fillets, cut into 2" pieces

SERVES: 6

CREAMY FISH CHOWDER

In a stock pot, render salt pork until medium brown. Stir with a wooden spoon to keep from burning. Add butter and heat until butter bubbles. Add onions, celery, and sauté until onions are transparent. Add flour and stir well with a wooden spoon to pick up the fat. Cook on low heat for 3 minutes. Add broth and stir to combine. Let simmer on low heat for 20 minutes. Add potatoes, thyme, Worcestershire sauce, pepper and simmer for 10 minutes more. Put milk and Half-and-Half in a bowl. With a large ladle, remove some of the broth and combine with the milk mixture to make the milk warm. Then slowly add warm milk to soup. Adding milk quickly will cause the soup to curdle.

Let soup simmer until potatoes are just tender. Add fish pieces. Cover and let steep for 5 minutes. Adjust seasoning with salt and pepper and serve with oyster crackers.

Chef John's Tips

- This recipe requires a firm fish to keep its shape in the broth.
- If you prefer a thicker chowder, sprinkle some instant potatoes on top of the broth and gently whisk so you do not mash the fish or vegetables.
- For additional flavor, add 1/2 cup sherry wine.

Creamy Fish Chowder Ingredients

- *1/2 cup salt pork or bacon (diced fine)*
- *2 Tbsp. butter*
- *2 cups white onions, cut into 1/2" cubes*
- *2 cups celery, cut into 1/4" slices*
- *1/3 cup flour*
- *1 quart clam or fish stock (see recipe)*
- *2 cups potatoes, peeled and cubed in 1/2" pieces*
- *1 Tbsp. fresh thyme or 1 1/2 tsp. dry thyme*
- *1 Tbsp. Worcestershire sauce*
- *1/8 tsp. black pepper, fresh cracked*
- *2 cups milk*
- *1 pint Half-and-Half*
- *4 cups boneless, skinless fish cubes*
- *1/4 tsp. salt*
- *1/8 tsp. black pepper, freshly ground*

SERVES: 8 to 10

FISH in a TIN POUCH

Preheat oven to 375°.

Cut peppers in half end to end. Remove seeds and stem. On a flat surface, lay out four large sheets of double-thick aluminum foil. In the center of each sheet, place a fish fillet. Season lightly with lemon pepper and top with potato slices, zucchini, carrots, onion slices, red peppers, thyme, lemon juice and a slab of butter.

Fold up foil to make a tight pouch, and bake in 375° oven for one hour. When carrots are tender, it is time to serve.

Chef John's Tips

- This is one of those time-tested recipes that just cannot be beat!

- This recipe is perfect for a campfire. Use double foil and turn the fish pouches often. Keep on the medium-heat side of fire.

- When cutting carrots and zucchini, it is important to make pieces 1/2 to 1″ thick and 3 to 4″ long. This helps in the stacking.

- The thicker the fish steak or fillet the better. If using tender fillet, place potatoes on bottom of stack first.

- Some of the simplest recipes are still the best. I was not a boy scout being a farm kid, but I made these fish bakes at 4-H camp.

Fish in a Tin Pouch Ingredients

- 2 red peppers
- 4 - 8 to 10 oz. salmon or lake trout fillets
  or steaks
- 1 tsp. lemon pepper seasoning
- 4 large potatoes, unpeeled and
  sliced 1/2" thick
- 4 zucchini, sliced 1/2" thick into 3
  long slabs
- 4 carrots, peeled and sliced 1/2" thick
  into 3 long slabs
- 2 large onions, sliced 1" thick
- 2 tsp. fresh thyme
- 4 tsp. fresh lemon juice
- 1/2 lb. butter, cut into 4 slabs

SERVES: 4

EASY PAN FISH CHIPS

Scale fish and leave the skin on. In a large skillet heat the oil until hot. Roll fish fillets in seasoned flour and shake off the excess. Add butter to oil. Place fish in oil, skin side down. Fry for 1 1/2 to 2 minutes. Turn gently and fry until golden brown. Fish will appear milky white and flake when done. Remove from pan and place on absorbent paper towels. Serve with lemon and kosher salt.

Chef John's Tips

- The reason for leaving the skin on is to help hold the fillets together. It is alright to remove the skin if you are in a hurry or too lazy to scale first!

Easy Pan Fish Chips
Ingredients

- 20 pan fish fillets of choice
- 1 Tbsp. vegetable oil
- 1 1/2 cups seasoned flour (see recipe)
- 2 Tbsp. clarified butter (see recipe)
- 1 lemon, cut into wedges
- salt to taste

SERVES: 4

BEER BATTERED FISH

Prepare fish fillets.

Pour beer in a bowl. Add 1 cup flour. Whisk smooth. Refrigerate until needed. Heat a deep fryer or electric skillet to 375°. Dredge fish pieces in seasoned flour and shake off excess flour. Dip in batter. Shake off excess batter. Fry in 375° oil until golden brown. Remove to a paper towel lined bowl. Sprinkle with your favorite seasoning.

Chef John's Tips

- This recipe works well because it does not contain salt. Salt will break down the frying oil, causing it to separate and burn.

- Add seasonings after frying the fish.

- Canola oil has a mild flavor and higher smoke point.

- For battered vegetables, use the same preparation with small vegetable pieces.

- For battered fruit, roll fruit in a shallow dish with 1 cup granulated sugar and 1 tsp. cinnamon after frying.

Beer Battered Fish Ingredients

- 6 to 8 boneless pan fish fillets or 4 to 6
  2"x 2" fish squares
- 12 oz. bottle or can of beer
- 1 cup all-purpose flour
- 1/4 cup seasoned flour (see recipe)
- 1 qt. vegetable oil for frying

SERVES: 4

FISH TACOS

Combine taco seasoning with flour. Place in a pie pan. Dredge fish cubes in seasoned flour mixture. Add Tabasco sauce to egg wash and combine. Dip floured cubes in egg wash and roll in cornmeal to create a thick crust. Place on a cornmeal dusted platter.

Preheat oven to 350°. Place taco shells in oven for 5 minutes to heat and crisp. Heat vegetable oil in a deep fryer or electric skillet to 375°. Deep fry fish until golden brown. Remove to a paper towel lined bowl.

To serve, place fried fish in taco shells and fill with taco fixings.

Chef John's Tips

- You may use any fresh or salt water fish with this recipe.
- Have a tray with cups of taco fixings ready. Let family or guests create their own favorite tacos.
- For burritos, simply wrap fish and fixings in soft tortilla shells.

Fish Taco Ingredients

- *4 cups boneless fish, cut into 1" cubes*
- *1 Tbsp. taco seasoning mix*
- *1 cup seasoned flour (see recipe)*
- *4 drops hot Tabasco sauce*
- *1 cup egg wash (see recipe)*
- *2 cups white or blue cornmeal*
- *10 to 12 taco shells*
- *3 cups vegetable oil*

TACO FIXINGS
- *4 cups shredded lettuce*
- *2 cups shredded cheese*
- *2 cups diced tomatoes*
- *1 cup diced dill pickles*
- *1 cup sliced black olives*
- *1/4 cup capers*
- *1/4 cup fresh cilantro*
- *4 sliced hot peppers*
- *1 cup guacamole*
- *1 cup sour cream*

SERVES: 4

GRILLED FISH T-BONE STEAKS with ANCHOVY CAPER BUTTER

Heat grill to medium hot. Brush grill and steaks with olive oil. Place fish steaks on grill. Cook for 3 minutes. Turn to mark with a crisscross pattern and grill for 3 more minutes. Turn steaks over and repeat grilling. When testing for doneness, test meat closest to the bone. When steaks are medium rare, splash with Worcestershire sauce and remove to warm serving platter. Cut a 1" slice of Anchovy Caper Butter and put on top of each steak. Serve with a wedge of lemon.

Chef John's Tips

- This is a great shore lunch.
- Boneless steaks and fillets work just as well as bone-in steaks.
- I bring anchovy caper butter with me in a double plastic bag in a small cooler or my beer cooler.

Grilled Fish T-Bone Steaks with Anchovy Caper Butter

Ingredients

- 2 Tbsp. olive oil
- 4- 10 oz. bone-in fish steaks
- 2 tsp. Worcestershire sauce
- Anchovy Caper Butter

SERVES: 4

GRILLED SALMON

Cut salmon into fillets or steaks. I like 10 oz. pieces. Brush or spray with olive oil. Place fillets skin side down on a medium hot grill. After 4 minutes gently lift fillets and route to make cross marks. Grill for an additional 3 minutes. Turn fillets over and repeat.

Fillets should be cooked to medium rare or at most medium done to keep moisture and flavor in.

To have best results, preheat grill. Brush rack with a wire brush and wipe off debris. Spray rack with a non-stick oil. Then place fish on grill. When grilling fish, I stay at the grill until fish are done.

I also like to grill onion slices 1/2″ thick and red peppers the same as fish.

Serve with fresh lemon.

Grilled Salmon Ingredients

- 4 Salmon fillets or steaks (10 oz. pieces)
- olive oil
- fresh lemon

SERVES: 4

FARMWIFE FISH FILLETS

Combine flour, dry mustard, salt and white pepper. Sift out any lumps.

Preheat oven to 350°.

In a heavy pan heat butter to a fast bubble. Coat fillets in flour mix and shake off excess flour. Add to pan and brown. Turn and bake in a 350° oven 5 minutes or until fillets are tender. They should be flaky and milky white. Place fish fillets on a warm serving plate. Add lemon juice, dill weed and dill pickles to butter mixture. Bring to a boil. Place fillets on top of 2 slices fresh bread and top with dill butter sauce.

Chef John's Tips

- Finish the fish in the oven to keep fillets tender and moist.
- Sour dough bread or homemade bread is the best.
- I use capers instead of dill pickles.
- I substitute white rice or wild rice for bread slices.

Farmwife Fish Fillets
Ingredients

- 1 cup flour
- 1 tsp. dry mustard
- 1 tsp. salt
- 1/2 tsp. white pepper
- 2 Tbsp. butter
- 4 to 6 medium fish fillets, skinned
- 1/2 cup fresh lemon juice
- 1 tsp. fresh dill weed, minced
- 2 tsp. dill pickles, diced into 1/4" cubes
- 8 slices fresh bread

SERVES: 4

ITALIAN STUFFED FISH

Heat 2 tablespoons olive oil. Add onions and sauté until tender. Add mushrooms, red wine and cook for 2 minutes on low heat. Place spaghetti sauce of choice in a bowl and add cooked onions and mushrooms. Combine well.

Line a baking pan with aluminum foil. Brush with olive oil or butter. Put seasoned flour in a large bag. Add fillets and gently coat fillets.

Place a fillet, fat or skin side down on the baking pan. In the other fillet, cut a slit in the center leaving at least 2" attached on both ends. Place sliced fillet on top of other fish fillet. Spread open the center and fill with spaghetti mixture.

Let remaining sauce run over the top of the fish and on the pan. Sprinkle with Parmesan cheese and basil and bake at 375° for 20 - 30 minutes or until fillet is flaky at the thickest part. Remove and serve.

Chef John's Tips

- You may top with sliced hot peppers.

Italian Stuffed Fish
Ingredients

- *2 Tbsp. olive oil*
- *1/2 cup onions, diced in 1/2" pieces*
- *1 cup fresh mushrooms, cut in fourths*
- *1/2 cup red wine*
- *1 pint mushroom spaghetti sauce*
- *1 1/2 cups seasoned flour for dredging*
  (see recipe)
- *2 skinless fish fillets, about*
  2 to 3 pounds each
- *1/4 cup Parmesan cheese*
- *fresh basil*

SERVES: 4

FRIED WHOLE PAN FISH

Scale and remove head and insides from fish. Remove the dorsal fin and leave the tail on. Wash fish well in cold salted water. Pat dry.

Heat vegetable oil to 375°. Add butter. Roll fish in seasoned flour and shake off excess. Place fish in pan and brown to a golden color. Turn and brown on the other side. When fish are done, remove to a plate lined with absorbent paper towels. Serve with fresh lemon.

Chef John's Tips

- My mother always made pan fish this way on the farm. She served them with her hash browns (see recipe). It is my favorite recipe for pan fish.

- Have a side dish handy for fish bones. My father, Big Cully, calls this a bone jar. Advise your guests that taking the time to remove bones before eating is well worth the extra time and effort.

Fried Whole Pan Fish
Ingredients

- 12 pan fish
- salted water, 1 tsp. salt per quart
- 1 1/2 cups vegetable oil
- 1/4 cup butter
- 1 1/2 cups seasoned flour (see recipe)
- lemon for squeezing

SERVES: 4

FISH CHILI

In a heavy soup pot, heat oil until hot. Add onions, garlic, celery and sauté until tender. Add all remaining ingredients except fish and simmer on low heat for 30 minutes. Add fish. Cover and cook 5 minutes on low. Serve gently being careful to not break up fish.

Chef John's Tips

- For this recipe, I prefer to use salmon, lake trout or firm salt water fish to keep pieces in tact.

- It is necessary to use a stronger flavored fish so the fish will not be overwhelmed by the chili powder.

- For garnish, mix 1 cup sour cream with 2 tsp. chili powder. Put a dollop on top of the chili.

- Shredded Farmer's cheese sprinkled on top of the sour cream adds a nice touch.

- If you feel adventuresome, add a few shrimp or scallops to the chili.

- Peel celery with a potato peeler, then slice.

Fish Chili Ingredients

- 1 Tbsp. olive oil
- 1 1/2 cups red onions, chopped 1/2"
- 2 cloves fresh garlic, minced fine
- 1 cup celery, peeled, cut in 1/4" slices
- 3 cups canned diced tomatoes and juice
- 1 cup dry red wine
- 1 can butter beans, drained
- 1 can chili beans
- 1/4 cup chili powder
- 1 Tbsp. fresh cilantro, chopped fine
- 1 tsp. salt
- 1/4 tsp. black pepper
- 1/4 tsp. cinnamon
- 1/2 tsp. cumin
- 1/2 tsp. allspice
- 2 jalapeño peppers, stem and seeds
  removed, diced 1/4"
- 4 cups fish, cubed in 1" pieces

SERVES: 8 to 10

FISH in a RED SEA BAG

Preheat oven to 350°. Sprinkle fish fillets with Cajun seasoning and pepper. Top with a slice of Provolone cheese and ham. Roll up into cylinders. Set aside.

Remove the tops and seeds of the red peppers. Set tops aside. Place one fish fillet cylinder in each red pepper. Top with 1/2 teaspoon olive oil. In between fish cylinder and pepper, put red onion pieces to fill pepper. Top with chicken stock and pretzel crumbs.

Place remaining red onion pieces, green pepper, carrots and red pepper pieces on the bottom of a casserole dish. Place filled red peppers on vegetables. Cover and bake in a 350° oven for 1 1/2 hours. When fish is tender, remove from oven. Serve with vegetables and liquid from casserole.

Chef John's Tips

- Green peppers can be used in place of red peppers.

- I was a cook and baker on a submarine in the Navy so it if looked like a bag, it must be a sea bag!

- I sometimes substitute corned beef or pastrami for the ham.

Fish in a Red Sea Bag Ingredients

- 4 - 4 to 6 oz. fish fillets
- 2 tsp. Cajun seasoning
- 1/4 tsp. pepper
- 4 slices Provolone or Swiss cheese
- 4 ham slices, 1/8" thick
- 4 large red peppers
- 2 tsp. olive oil
- 1 cup red onion, diced into 1/4" pieces
- 1 cup chicken stock
- 1 cup mustard pretzel crumbs
- 1 green pepper, diced into 1/4" pieces
- 1 cup carrots, diced into 1/4" pieces

SERVES: 4

FISH STIR FRY

Peel and cut vegetables. In a wok or heavy sauté pan heat oil until smoke hot. Add vegetables and cook for 3 minutes turning gently to keep from burning. Combine cornstarch, soy sauce, fresh ginger and chicken stock. Add to vegetables and bring to a simmer. Add fish, tossing gently and cook until fish is tender and sauce is clear. Remove and serve over white rice.

Chef John's Tips

- This is my favorite recipe for bluefish or bass.
- Firmer fish fillets work best for this dish.
- Leaving the skin on the fillets helps keep the fish pieces intact.
- The vegetables look and cook best if sliced Chinese style or on the bias.
- This is an easy campfire dish when made in a heavy iron pan. The hotter the fire the better.

Fish Stir Fry
Ingredients

- 3 cups fish fillets, sliced into finger sized
  pieces, skin on
- 1 cup onions, sliced 1/4"
- 1 cup carrots, sliced 1/4" thick on the bias
- 1 cup celery, sliced 1/4" thick on the bias
- 1 cup red pepper, sliced 1/4" thick, 3" long
- 1 cup fresh mushrooms, sliced 1/4"
- 1 1/2 Tbsp. vegetable oil or saffron oil
- 1 Tbsp. cornstarch
- 1 Tbsp. soy sauce
- 1 tsp. fresh ginger root, minced fine
- 2 cups chicken stock, fish stock or clam
  broth (see fish stock recipe)
- 4 cups cooked white rice (see recipe)

SERVES: 4

POACHED FILLETS *with* CUCUMBER SAUCE

Place all poaching liquid and vegetable ingredients in a medium-sized sauce pan and simmer on low heat for 10 minutes. Bring to a boil. Add fish fillets. Remove from heat and cover for 8 to 10 minutes. Remove fillets very carefully with a slotted spoon.

To serve, place fish on steamed white rice and top with matchstick vegetables. Place Cucumber Sauce in a ramekin and serve on the side.

Chef John's Tips

- For larger fish, cut boneless fish fillets into 4" squares. Fish should not be over 1/2" thick.
- If you are like me, (short on patience) cut vegetables into 1/4" slices.

Poached Fillets with Cucumber Sauce Ingredients

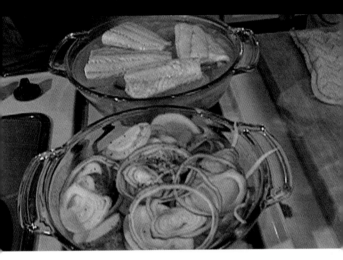

Poaching liquid and vegetables

- *2 cups water*
- *1/2 cup onions, matchstick size 3" long*
- *1/4 cup carrots, matchstick size 3" long*
- *1/4 cup celery, matchstick size 3" long*
- *1 bay leaf*
- *1/2 cup white wine*
- *1/2 lemon, seeds removed*
- *6 peppercorns*
- *1/4 tsp. salt*

- *12 boneless perch or pan fish fillets*
- *4 cups steamed rice (see Long Grained White Rice recipe)*
- *2 cups Cucumber Sauce (see recipe)*

SERVES: 4

THE FISH is in the BAG

Preheat oven to 375°. Cut fish fillets into 1 1/2"cubes. Combine instant potatoes, Parmesan cheese, thyme, salt and pepper together in a shallow bowl and toss gently. Put fish in mixture and coat well.

Place vegetables, lemon juice and melted butter in an oven roaster bag. Shake gently to combine. Remove fillets from dry mixture. Add remaining dry mixture to vegetable bag and gently toss again. Place bag in a baking pan or Dutch oven. Top the vegetable mixture with fish. Close bag and fasten tight. Put a slit in the top of the bag and bake at 375° for 20 minutes. Remove from oven and serve.

Chef John's Tips

- I use a roasting bag in a Dutch oven for camp cooking. Add 1 1/2 cups water to Dutch oven to keep bag from burning to the bottom.

- It is very important to use plastic roaster bags. They are made to be used in high heat. Do not use a common plastic bag.

- If no plastic roaster bag is available, make a foil pouch.

- The vegetables need to be cubed small to be tender when fish are done.

- The liquid from vegetables and fish makes the sauce.

The Fish is in the Bag
Ingredients

- 4 - 8 to 10 oz. fish fillets
- 1/2 cup instant potatoes
- 1/2 cup Parmesan cheese
- 2 tsp. fresh thyme
- 1 tsp. salt
- 1/8 tsp. white pepper
- Medium to large oven bag
- 2 cups potatoes, sliced 1/4", skins on
- 1 cup red onions, diced into 1/4" cubes
- 1 cup carrots, diced into 1/4" slices
- 1 cup celery, peeled and diced into1/4" slices
- 2 tsp. lemon juice
- 1 1/2 Tbsp. butter, melted

SERVES: 4

FISH CASINO

In a large frying pan, heat butter to a fast bubble. Dredge fish in seasoned flour and shake off excess flour. Place fish in butter and fry until golden brown. Gently turn and reduce heat and cook for 2 to 3 minutes or until tender.

While fish are cooking, heat olive oil in a medium frying pan. Add peppers and scallions. Sauté for 1 minute. Add capers, cooked bacon and Worcestershire sauce. Combine gently. Remove cooked fish fillets and place on a warm serving platter. Top fish fillets with casino mixture and serve with lemon wedges.

Chef John's Tips

- This is an outstanding recipe for all fish fillets and steaks.

- You may have noticed that this is the only recipe where I use green peppers. I am not a fan of green peppers and rarely use them in recipes.

- When asked what I don't like, my answer is always green peppers, peanut butter, black jelly beans and short kisses!

Fish Casino
Ingredients

- *4 - 8 to 10 oz. fish fillets*
- *2 Tbsp. butter*
- *1/2 cup seasoned flour (see recipe)*
- *1 Tbsp. olive oil*
- *1/2 cup red peppers, diced 1/4"*
- *1/2 cup green peppers, diced 1/4"*
- *1/2 cup scallions, sliced 1/4"*
- *1 Tbsp. capers, drained*
- *1/2 cup cooked bacon, diced 1/4"*
- *1 tsp. Worcestershire sauce*
- *1 whole lemon, cut into 4 wedges*

SERVES: 4

FISH BLT TRIPLE DECKERS

Grill or fry fish fillets. Place avocados in a bowl with lemon juice. Combine tartar sauce and capers. Remove stems and slice tomatoes. Sprinkle with Kosher salt and grind fresh black pepper to taste over the top of tomatoes.

Toast bread golden brown and lay bread slices on a cotton towel in lines 3 slices tall.

To make triple decker: Spread each bread slice with a generous amount of tartar sauce. On two slices place a leaf of lettuce. Top one lettuce leaf with 2 tomato slices and 2 pieces of bacon. Top the other lettuce leaf with fish and avocado slices.

Now the fun part. Top the bacon/lettuce/tomato piece with the slice that has tartar sauce on it (sauce side down). Spread dry side with more tartar sauce and add a lettuce leaf. Turn fish slice over top of middle slice to make the 3rd deck. Put 2 long picks in the sandwich to fasten shut. Cut in half. Serve with a Kosher dill pickle.

Chef John's Tips

- It is a whopper to see, but even more fun to eat.
- The way to keep all 3 decks together is to spread sauce on dry side of middle slice.
- Crisp iceberg lettuce may be used in place of leaf lettuce.
- If you are not a bacon lover, use turkey or corned beef.

Fish BLT Triple Deckers
Ingredients

- *4 - 6 to 8 oz. large fish fillets or boneless steaks*
- *2 avocados, peeled and sliced into 1/2" slices*
- *1 Tbsp. fresh lemon juice*
- *1 cup tartar sauce (see recipe)*
- *1 Tbsp. capers*
- *2 large fresh tomatoes, cut into 1/2" thick slices*
- *1 tsp. Kosher salt*
- *fresh black pepper to taste*
- *12 slices sour dough bread*
- *1 head leaf lettuce*
- *8 slices crisp cooked bacon*

SERVES: 4

GRAVLAX

Fillet fish. Lightly run a flat hand over inside of the fillet to find pin bones. Remove pin bones with a needle-nose pliers.

Lay salmon fillets skin side down on a cotton dish towel or double thick piece of cheese cloth. Combine all ingredients. Spread evenly over both salmon fillets. Place 1 fillet over the other skin side up. Roll tightly in cloth and place in a flat baking pan. Place a flat pan over the top and add 5 lb. of weight distributing the weight evenly over the fillets. Refrigerate for 24 hours. Remove from refrigerator. Drain off excess liquid. Turn fish over and repeat the process for 3 more days.

To serve, remove salmon fillets from cloth. Brush off curing spices. Slice thinly on the bias. Serve with capers, shallots, sour cream and rye toasts.

For storage: Cut fillets in half. Place in double thick resealable plastic bag. Add 1 oz. vegetable oil to help keep fish soft. Freeze flat. Use fillet within 90 days.

Chef John's Tips

- If you are not a fan of juniper berries, leave them out.
- I made this in camp when I was in Alaska and kept the fish in a pit dug in the permafrost.

Gravlax Ingredients

- *1 - 6 to 8 lbs. salmon*
- *1/3 cup salt*
- *1/3 cup brown sugar*
- *3 Tbsp. fresh dill weed or 1 Tbsp. dried dill weed*
- *2 Tbsp. black pepper, coarsely ground*
- *1/4 tsp. ground allspice*
- *2 tsp. juniper berries, mashed medium*

EACH FILLET SALMON SERVES: 6 to 8

CATFISH over GRITS

Combine flour and Cajun seasoning in a shallow bowl.

Heat oil hot in a large skillet. Dredge fish fillets in Cajun flour. Shake off excess flour. Place fish in skillet. Add butter. Brown fillets until golden. Turn. Slide fillets to one side of the pan.

Add scallions, mushrooms and tarragon. Cook until mushrooms and scallions are tender. Add 1 tsp. Cajun seasoned flour to make a slightly thick sauce. Stir to combine. Add shrimp, salt, pepper, balsamic vinegar and Worcestershire sauce. Bring to a boil. Remove from heat. Cover and let steep for 5 minutes. Place a large mound of grits in the center of a dinner plate. Make an indentation in the center of the grits. Top with catfish, vegetables and shrimp sauce.

Chef John's Tips

- Catfish fillets should not be more than 1/2" thick. If they are too thick, slice them in half.

Catfish over Grits
Ingredients

- 3 cups catfish fillets, cut in 2" squares, 1/2" thick
- 1/2 cup flour
- 1 Tbsp. Cajun seasoning
- 1 Tbsp. vegetable oil
- 1 Tbsp. butter
- 1/4 cup scallions, chopped 1/4" rounds
- 2 cups fresh mushrooms, sliced 1/4" thick
- 1 Tbsp. fresh tarragon, chopped medium
- 2 cups peeled uncooked shrimp
- 1/2 tsp. salt
- 1/4 tsp. ground black pepper
- 1 Tbsp. balsamic vinegar
- 1 tsp. Worcestershire sauce
- 4 cups grits

SERVES: 4

FISHERMEN'S QUICHE

Preheat oven to 375°.

Make pie crust dough. Roll out dough to 1/8″ thickness and place in a 9 to 10 inch pie plate. Place onions, cheeses, fish, mushrooms, red peppers and dill pickles in the pie pan. In a bowl, whisk the eggs, yolks, Half-and-Half, thyme, salt and pepper to a smooth liquid and pour over filling. This will be a very full pie. Put in the oven on a baking sheet or cookie pan.

Place in a 375° oven for about 45 minutes or until set. Let stand 10 minutes. Serve with salsa.

Chef John's Tips

- All smoked fish works well with this recipe.
- If you are feeling like you own Park Place or Boardwalk, serve with sour cream and caviar.
- For ease of time, it is just fine to use a premade frozen pie crust.
- This is one of my favorite breakfast dishes.

Fishermen's Quiche
Ingredients

- 1- 9" pie crust (see recipe)
- 1/4 cup green onions
- 1/2 cup Farmer's cheese
- 1/2 cup Cheddar cheese, shredded
- 1 1/2 cups fish fillets, diced 1/2" thick
- 1 cup fresh mushrooms, diced
  1/2" thick
- 1/2 cup red peppers, diced 1/2" thick
- 1/4 cup diced dill pickles, diced 1/4" thick
- 4 eggs
- 2 egg yolks
- 1 1/2 cups Half-and-Half
- 1/4 tsp. thyme
- 1 tsp. salt
- 1/4 tsp. pepper

SERVES: 4

CHEF JOHN'S FISH HEAD SOUP

Fillet fish and store for future use. Save fish bones, skins with scales on and heads. Remove eyes and gills and discard. Remove entrails and discard. Wash fish bones, skins and heads. Place in a cheesecloth with sachet bag ingredients. Tie end with a string at least 2 feet long. Make sure not to tie bag tight as room is needed to let liquid in.

Put the cold water in a large heavy pot. Place the wrapped fish bones, vegetables, peppercorns, salt and dill seeds in water. Simmer on medium heat for 45 minutes. Remove bone bag letting all liquid run back into pot. Discard bones and heads. Rinse out cloth. Dry and keep for another time.

Add potatoes, white wine and simmer for 15 minutes. Remove from heat. Add fish. Cover and let steep for 4 to 5 minutes. Taste for flavor. It may need more salt or pepper. Gently serve in large mugs or bowls.

Chef John's Tips

- This is my favorite soup recipe. Don't let the name discourage you. It is a nice break on a fishing trip from fried fish

- After adding the fish it is important NOT to return the liquid to a boil. It overcooks the fish and breaks the pieces into small flakes

- Of course if you are a flake, boil away!

Chef John's Fish Head Soup Ingredients

- 3 lbs. fish bones, skins, heads
- 1 sachet bag (see recipe)
- 5 quarts cold water
- 3 cups onions, 1" cubes
- 3 cups carrots, 1/2" slices
- 3 cups celery, 1/4" slices
- 2 cups mushrooms, whole
- 1/2 tsp. black peppercorns, whole
- 1 Tbsp. salt
- 2 tsp. dill seeds
- 3 cups potatoes, skins on, cut in 1" cubes
- 2 cups dry white wine
- 4 cups fish fillets, 2" wide slices

SERVES: 4 to 6

SKILLET FISH STEW

In an iron skillet or Dutch oven, cook bacon until light brown. Do not overcook. Add onions, carrots, celery, peppers and cook until onions are tender. Stir with a wooden spoon to keep from burning. Add flour and stir to pick up bacon drippings. Cook for 3 minutes. Add beer, water, potatoes, ketchup, thyme, dill, salt & pepper. Stir gently to combine. Simmer soup for 20 minutes. Add fish. Remove from heat. Let stand covered for 5 minutes and serve.

Chef John's Tips

- Ketchup has vinegar and spices and if not overused, it adds a nice flavor to the stew.

- If you are not a bacon fan, use 1/4 cup olive oil.

- I also add baking powder dumplings. (See recipe.)

Skillet Fish Stew
Ingredients

- 6 slices raw bacon, diced 1/2"
- 1 cup onions, diced 1/2"
- 1 cup carrots, diced 1/2"
- 1 cup celery, diced 1/2"
- 1 cup red peppers, diced 1/4"
- 1 Tbsp. flour
- 12 oz. can beer
- 3 cups water
- 2 raw potatoes, skins on, diced 1/2" thick
- 1 cup ketchup
- 1 tsp. thyme
- 1 tsp. dill
- 1 tsp. salt
- black pepper to taste
- 3 cups fresh fish, cut in 2" cubes, skins on

SERVES: 8 to 10

LEMON EGG DROP and GINGER FISH SOUP

With a sharp potato peeler remove the yellow skin from a lemon in one piece. To avoid a bitter flavor, remove excess white membrane from inside of skin.

In a soup pot, place white wine, clam broth, chicken stock, garlic and ginger. Bring to a full boil. Let boil vigorously for 5 minutes. Reduce heat. Add onions, mushrooms, lemon zest and peppercorns.

Simmer for 10 minutes. Break eggs into a bowl. Add soy sauce. Whisk to a smooth liquid. Bring soup back to a boil. Add eggs through a colander while stirring broth. Remove from heat. Add fish and spinach leaves. Cover and let steep for 5 minutes. Check fish for doneness. Serve in large soup platters.

Chef John's Tips

- This is a great soup for the kids.
- Pan fish fillets are the best fish choice for this recipe.
- If you don't have Szechuan peppercorns, use black or white peppercorns.
- You may also add a few shrimp, scallops or oysters with the fillets.
- The reason for adding eggs through a strainer with the liquid moving is to keep eggs from forming large lumps. Eggs should look wispy in the soup.
- This is a great soup to make at camp over an open fire.

Lemon Egg Drop and Ginger Fish Soup Ingredients

- zest of one small lemon
- 1/2 cup dry white wine
- 1 cup clam broth
- 3 cups chicken stock
- 2 cloves garlic, minced fine
- 1 Tbsp. fresh ginger, peeled, diced 1/4"
- 1/2 cup green onions, sliced 1/4"
- 2 cups fresh mushrooms, sliced 1/4"
- 6 Szechuan peppercorns
- 4 eggs
- 1 Tbsp. soy sauce
- 3 cups fish fillets
- 2 cups fresh spinach leaves, whole

SERVES: 4 to 6

FISH BURGERS

Preheat oven to 350°.

In a skillet heat 1 Tbsp. butter to a fast bubble. Add scallions and celery. Cook until celery is light green and tender, about 1 to 2 minutes. Place in a large mixing bowl. Let cool for 10 minutes. Add salt, pepper, thyme, horseradish, Worcestershire sauce, fish and eggs to cooked celery and onion mixture. Combine well. Gently stir to make a paste. Sprinkle bread crumbs on top. Combine by hand to make a firm mixture. If mixture is too loose, add more bread crumbs a few at a time.

To make fish patties, fill a coffee cup with mixture. Press firm and place in a pan coated with seasoned flour. Roll fish patty in flour and form into desired shape. Place in refrigerator until chilled and firm.

Place a skillet on stove over medium heat. Put in 1 tablespoon butter and heat. Gently add patties. Do not over crowd. Cook until bottoms are golden brown. Turn with a wide spatula and brown the other side. Transfer patties to a cookie sheet and bake in a preheated 350° oven for 10 minutes or until patties are hot and firm all the way through. Serve on a roll with your favorite cheese and tartar sauce.

Chef John's Tips

- If the mix is too loose, the patties will flatten out when cooking. If the mix is too firm, the patties will crack and be dry.

Fish Burgers Ingredients

- 2 Tbsp. butter
- 1/2 cup scallions, cut into 1/4" cubes
- 1 cup celery, peeled and diced into
  1/4" cubes
- 1 tsp. Kosher salt
- 1/4 tsp. black pepper
- 1 Tbsp. fresh thyme leaves or 1 tsp.
  dry thyme
- 1 Tbsp. horseradish, squeezed dry
- 2 tsp. Worcestershire sauce
- 4 cups boneless fish fillets, cut into
  1/4" cubes
- 2 eggs beaten until frothy
- 1 cup fresh whole wheat bread crumbs
  (see fresh bread crumbs recipe)
- seasoned flour (see recipe)
- 1/2 cup tartar sauce (see recipe)

SERVES: 4

FISH SALAD

To make cold fish, poach boneless, skinless fillets in fish or chicken stock for 8 minutes and cool in refrigerator. Dice cooked fish into large pieces. Be sure to remove bones. Chop hard boiled eggs into coarse pieces. In a bowl, place dill, mayonnaise, sour cream, lemon juice, Worcestershire sauce, sugar, salt and pepper. Mix well. Peel celery with a potato peeler and dice into 1/4" pieces. Add eggs, celery and fish to mayonnaise base. Combine gently.

Pick tulips and remove pistils and stems. Place tulips in cold, salted water. Let sit for 5 minutes. Remove tulips and gently shake dry. On 4 plates place 1/4 head of leaf lettuce, place 3 tulips on top and fill with fish salad. Serve with a sweet pickle, piece of melon and soft roll.

Chef John's Tips

- If you have leftover fried or baked fish, make sure to remove excess breading.

- Prior to dicing celery, peel with potato peeler to remove celery strings.

- Of course, I don't serve fish salad in tulips on a fishing trip with my pals. I make monster fish salad sandwiches on sour dough bread or burger buns.

- If I did use tulips on a fly-in trip, I would never admit it.

Fish Salad Ingredients

- *2 cups cold cooked fish*
- *2 hard boiled eggs, chopped*
- *1 tsp. fresh dill weed, chopped*
- *1/2 cup mayonnaise*
- *1/4 cup sour cream*
- *1 tsp. lemon juice*
- *1 tsp. Worcestershire sauce*
- *2 tsp. sugar*
- *Pinch of salt and white pepper*
- *1/2 cup peeled celery, diced 1/4" thick*
- *12 tulips*
- *1 head leaf lettuce*

SERVES: 4

FISH REUBENS

Preheat oven to 375°.

Lightly coat fish fillets with seasoned flour. Dip in egg wash. Shake off excess and coat with pumpernickel crumbs.

Heat a skillet with clarified butter. Add fish fillets and brown. Turn fish fillets. Remove from heat. Top each fillet with 1 Tbsp. Thousand Island dressing and 2 pieces Swiss cheese. Place skillet in a 375° oven for 8 to 10 minutes until cheese turns light brown and starts to bubble. Top each fillet with 1/2 cup warmed Sweet Kraut.

Chef John's Tips

- This is an excellent way to prepare strong flavored fish like bass, blue fish and lake trout.

- If you are not fond of pumpernickel bread, use your favorite kind of bread.

- I sometimes use fried red onions instead of kraut.

Fish Reubens Ingredients

- 4 - 6 to 8 oz. skinless fillets
- 1/3 cup seasoned flour (see recipe)
- 1/2 cup egg wash (see recipe)
- 2 cups fresh pumpernickel bread crumbs
  (see bread crumb recipe)
- 1 1/2 Tbsp. clarified butter (see recipe)
- 1/3 cup Thousand Island dressing
- 8 slices Swiss cheese
- 2 cups warmed Sweet Kraut, drained

SERVES: 4

SKILLET POACHED EGGS and FILLETS in TOMATO SALSA

In a large iron skillet or Dutch oven heat olive oil. Add onions, garlic and red pepper and cook until onions are tender. Add red wine, salsa, cilantro and pepper. Bring to a boil. Add trout fillets and place around the edges of the pan. Place the eggs in the center of the skillet. Return to a simmer for 5 minutes. Remove from heat and cover 2 to 3 minutes or until eggs are cooked to your liking. With a large spoon remove fish, eggs and sauce. Place on a tortilla-shell lined plate.

Chef John's Tips

- The trout fillets will cook very quickly.

- Any thin boneless fish fillets will work in this recipe.

- I like to add a little sour cream to this dish.

- The tortilla shell is not only excellent with fish, it covers the plate and helps cut down on the dishwashing.

Skillet Poached Eggs and Fillets in Tomato Salsa

- 2 Tbsp. olive oil
- 1/2 cup onions, diced 1/4" thick
- 2 cloves garlic, diced fine
- 1 large red pepper, diced 1/4" thick
- 1/2 cup red wine
- 1 1/2 cups tomato salsa
- 1/3 cup cilantro, chopped coarse
  (fresh only)
- fresh black pepper to taste
- 4 - 4 to 6 oz. trout fillets
- 8 large eggs
- 4 large soft tortilla sheets

SERVES: 4

FISH PICCATA

Combine flour, salt, paprika and white pepper together and place in a pie pan.

In a large skillet heat oil until hot. Lightly coat fish fillets with flour mix. Shake off excess. Lay fish fillets skin side down in hot oil. Sauté until skins start to turn golden brown. Gently turn. Sauté about 1 1/2 to 2 minutes. Place on a warm platter. Cover with aluminum foil to keep hot.

Add shallots to the skillet. Stir with wooden spoon. When shallots become transparent, add flour, lemon juice, white and Marsala wine. Whisk smooth and bring to a rolling boil. Add capers and boil for 3 minutes. Remove from heat. Stir in whole butter. Spoon sauce over fillets. Garnish with sprigs of fresh tarragon.

Chef John's Tips

- This is a classic sauce.
- For a richer variation, add 2 tablespoons of heavy cream when adding the capers.
- If Marsala wine is not available, substitute cream sherry.
- It is important to add whole butter last. It adds richness to the sauce.

Fish Piccata Ingredients

- *1/4 cup flour*
- *1/2 tsp. salt*
- *1/4 tsp. paprika*
- *1/8 tsp. white pepper*
- *1 1/2 Tbsp. light colored olive oil*
- *4 - 6 to 8 oz. fish fillets, skins on*
- *1/4 cup shallots, diced 1/4"*
- *2 tsp. flour*
- *1 Tbsp. fresh lemon juice*
- *1 cup dry white wine*
- *1/4 cup Marsala wine*
- *1 Tbsp. drained capers*
- *1 Tbsp. whole butter*

SERVES: 4

TRADITIONAL BREADED FISH FILLETS

Coat fish fillets in seasoned flour. Shake off excess flour. Dip in egg wash and shake off excess. Dredge fish fillets in fresh bread crumbs. In an electric fry pan or deep fryer, heat vegetable oil to 375°. Fry fish in hot oil until brown and crisp. Remove and place in a paper towel lined platter. Splash with lemon juice. Serve with tartar sauce.

Chef John's Tips

- This tried and true recipe can be made with many variations.
- Use different kinds of bread when making bread crumbs.
- Add your favorite hot sauce to the egg wash.
- Add your favorite spices to the flour.

Traditional Breaded Fish Fillet Ingredients

- 8 - 4 to 6 oz. boneless fish fillets
- 1 cup seasoned flour (see recipe)
- 1 cup egg wash (see recipe)
- 2 cups fresh bread crumbs (see recipe)
- 1 1/2 cups vegetable oil
- 2 tsp. lemon juice
- tartar sauce (see recipe)

SERVES: 4

YELLOW CORNMEAL and PARMESAN CATFISH

Place seasoned flour in a pie pan. Mix Parmesan cheese, cornmeal and parsley flakes in another pie pan. Combine eggs and milk in a shallow bowl. Whisk mixture to a froth. Heat oil in an electric fry pan to 375°. When oil is hot, add butter. Dredge fish in flour mixture. Shake off excess flour. Dip fish in egg wash then roll in cornmeal mixture. Shake off excess cornmeal and place fish fillets in hot oil. Brown on one side for about 2 minutes, being careful not to overcook. Turn and cook until done. Remove from oil and place on paper towel lined dish. Lightly splash with lemon juice and dust with your favorite seasoning.

Chef John's Tips

- This is an excellent breading for deep frying all varieties of fish fillets.

- The oil needs to be at 375°. If it is too hot, the fish will burn. If it is too cold, the fish will absorb too much oil. I test the hotness of the oil with a slice of raw potato. If the oil is too cold, the potato will not bubble. If the oil is too hot, the slice of potato will turn dark brown after 30 seconds.

- To add some spiciness, fry chili peppers after removing stems and seeds. When in camp, I use a deep frying pan with 2-3 inches of vegetable oil.

Yellow Cornmeal and Parmesan Catfish Ingredients

- 1 cup seasoned flour (see recipe)
- 1 cup freshly grated Parmesan cheese
- 1 cup cornmeal (yellow or white)
- 1 Tbsp. parsley flakes
- 2 eggs
- 3/4 cup milk
- 2 cups vegetable oil
- 1/4 cup butter
- 4 catfish fillets, skinned and cut into 5" slabs
- 1 Tbsp. fresh lemon juice
- 1 tsp. seasoning of choice (Cajun, taco or lemon pepper)

SERVES: 4

POACHED FISH ROLL-UPS with ASPARAGUS & CARROTS

In a large sauce pot, heat water, wine, salt and lemon to a brisk boil. Add asparagus, carrot strips and return water to a boil. With a skimmer, remove vegetables immediately and plunge into ice water to stop the cooking process. Keep vegetable liquid. When vegetables are well chilled, roll 4 asparagus pieces and 3 carrot pieces in fillets skin side out. Wrap two 1/2" thick strips of yellow pepper around outside of fish roll. Fasten with a long toothpick. Place fish roll-up seam side down in vegetable liquid. Cover and simmer on low for 15 minutes.

Remove pot from heat. Test for doneness. When fish is tender, remove from broth with a slotted spoon. Serve fish on steamed or fried rice seam side down.

Chef John's Tips

- Two things are very important with this recipe. First, do not over blanch asparagus and carrots. They also must be chilled in ice water immediately and removed as soon as they are chilled.

- Second, when poaching fish roll-ups remember vegetables are already cooked. When fish is tender, the vegetables will be hot.

- To create pepper strips, set pepper stem end up. Remove stem and slice across whole pepper making horseshoe strips 1/2" wide. The end pieces may be poached and served.

Poached Fish Roll-ups with Asparagus & Carrots Ingredients

- 2 cups cold water
- 1/2 cup white wine
- 1/2 tsp. salt
- 8 whole cloves stuck into outside of a whole lemon
- 12 large asparagus spears, cut in half
- 8 carrot strips, 1/3" thick and 3" long
- 4 - 8 to 10 oz. boneless fish fillets
- 2 large yellow peppers, cut into 1/2" strips
- 4 cups Rice Pilaf (see recipe)

SERVES: 4

BOILED SHORE LUNCH

First you have to catch the fish. This is the hard part. Then clean, scale and cut into fish steaks.

Place potatoes, carrots, onions, rice, salt, thyme, bay leaves, pepper and garlic in a large pot with cold water. Cover and bring to a boil over hot camp fire for about 45 minutes. Add fish and pickles and simmer 5 minutes. With help, remove the pot from fire. Leaving the cover on, drain the liquid completely. Remove cover. Top fish with slabs of butter. Let vegetables and fish steam off. For each hungry fisherman place 2 potatoes, 1 onion, 1 pickle and 2 pieces of fish on a plate. Top with butter/rice mixture.

Chef John's Tips

- This recipe is intended for lake trout, salmon, white fish, striped bass, cod and scrod. It is an excellent change after eating fried fish for a week.

- When draining liquid, be careful not to pour out rice when draining off the water. This is difficult to do, but very important.

- For backyard entertaining, cook over a gas grill or outdoor fire.

Boiled Shore Lunch Ingredients

- 8 to 10 - 3" thick fish steaks, scaled
- 8 medium red potatoes, skins on
- 8 whole carrots, peeled
- 4 small red onions, peeled
- 2 cups long grain rice
- 1 Tbsp. salt
- 1 Tbsp. thyme
- 3 bay leaves
- 1/2 tsp. black pepper
- 4 cloves garlic, whole
- 1 1/2 to 2 gallons cold water
- 4 large whole dill pickles
- 1/2 lb. butter

SERVES: 4

FISHBALLS

Cook potatoes. Drain and let steam off well and mash. Do not add any extra ingredients as it will make the potatoes too soft. Set aside to cool.

Dice fish fillets into very small pieces. In a small skillet, heat butter to a fast bubble. Add onions and sauté until tender. Do not brown. Add fish. Combine well. Remove from heat. Cover and let sit off the stove for 10 minutes. Place in a large mixing bowl. Add remaining ingredients except mashed potatoes and seasoned flour. Combine well. Add potatoes to make a dough. It should have the same consistency as mashed potatoes. If the consistency is too loose, add dry instant potatoes or more Parmesan cheese. Cover and place in a refrigerator to cool and firm. Form into walnut-sized balls. Roll in seasoned flour and shake off excess flour.

Heat an electric skillet to 375°. Fry 5 to 6 fishballs at one time. Do not over brown. Remove with a skimmer to a paper towel lined bowl. Season with celery salt or your favorite seasoning. Serve with scrambled eggs or as an appetizer.

Chef John's Tips

- You may substitute instant potatoes for mashed potatoes.

Fishballs Ingredients

- *2 cups mashed potatoes*
- *1 lb. skinless, boneless fish fillets*
- *1 Tbsp. butter*
- *1 cup red onions, diced fine*
- *1/4 tsp. black pepper*
- *2 eggs*
- *1 egg yolk*
- *1/4 tsp. salt*
- *1/4 tsp. lemon zest, shredded fine*
- *1 tsp. poultry seasoning*
- *1/2 cup Parmesan cheese*
- *4 drops Tabasco sauce*
- *1/2 cup seasoned flour (see recipe)*

SERVES: 4

WHOLE FISH GRILLED in APPLE BACON

Scale the fish well on both sides, back and belly. Remove insides, gills and eyes. With a vegetable brush lightly clean fish inside and out. Run cold water over fish inside and out. In cavity place potato slices, shallots, shredded apple, tarragon or thyme sprigs, lemon zest, lemon juice and sprinkle evenly with pepper. Make sure potatoes are inside fish. Wrap bacon around fish overlapping to form the crust. Do not wrap head and tail. Wrap tail in a double thick piece of foil to keep it from burning.

Heat grill medium hot. Place fish in fish rack. Brush fish lightly with vegetable oil. Set rack on grill. Turn every 4 to 5 minutes until bacon is brown and fish is tender, about 30 minutes. While grilling make sure there is not a flare up from dripping bacon fat and fish vegetable juices. The thickest part closest to the fish head takes the longest to cook. When testing for doneness, test meat closest to the bone. When cooked, place fish on a platter. Remove foil from tail. Slice into 2″ to 3″ slabs. When serving, remind guests about bones.

Chef John's Tips

- For a recipe variation, pour 1/4 cup barbecue sauce over shallots and potatoes once inside before wrapping with bacon. To roast in oven, set heat at 400° and bake for 30 to 35 minutes. Test often for doneness!

- If you don't have apple bacon, regular thick sliced bacon is alright to use.

in Apple Bacon
Ingredients

- 1 - 4 to 5 lbs. whole fish
- 1 cup boiled potatoes, sliced in 1/4" rounds
- 4 shallots, diced in 1/4" cubes
- 1 cup green apple, unpeeled and shredded
- 2 sprigs fresh tarragon or thyme
- 1/2 tsp. lemon zest, grated fine
- 1 tsp. lemon juice
- 1/8 tsp. fresh ground black pepper
- 1 to 1 1/2 lbs. apple bacon, sliced thick

SERVES: 4

BARBECUED FISH *with* SWEET POTATO MEDALLIONS

Wash and cut sweet potatoes into 1/2" thick rounds. Boil in salted water for 10 minutes. Drain off water and let potatoes steam off. Keep refrigerated until needed.

Heat grill to medium hot. Brush fish steaks and sweet potato slices with olive oil. Place fish and sweet potatoes on grill and cook for 3 minutes. Turn to make crisscross marks. Let cook 3 minutes more. Turn over. Brush tops with soft butter. Sprinkle with brown sugar and nutmeg mixture. Top with barbecue sauce. Shut lid and cook 3 to 4 minutes. When fish is medium rare, place fish steaks and sweet potatoes on a platter. Serve with lemon wedges.

Chef John's Tips

- If desired, mashed sweet potatoes can be made after removing from grill. Place potatoes in a bowl with 1 tablespoon butter and 1 tablespoon cream. Mash and serve under steaks.

- A great shore lunch item.

Barbecued Fish with Sweet Potato Medallions
Ingredients

- 4 small or 2 large sweet potatoes
- 4 - 8 to 10 oz. fish steaks
- 1/2 cup olive oil
- 1/4 cup butter
- 1/4 cup brown sugar
- 1/2 tsp. nutmeg (combined in brown sugar)
- 1 cup barbecue sauce of choice
- 4 lemon wedges

Serves: 4

GRILLED FISH KABOBS
that WORK

Cut fish into cubes and roll in seasoned flour in a pie plate.
Remove to a rack and let dry for 10 minutes. Lay bacon out
to temper. In a sauce pan heat water and salt to boiling. Add
red potatoes. Let boil for 10 minutes. Add whole shallots and
boil for 5 minutes. Drain potatoes and shallots into a
colander and let steam off. In a skillet, heat olive oil hot. Add
pepper cubes, zucchini slices, mushroom caps and sauté for
2 minutes. Add sherry. Turn and simmer for 2 minutes more.
Remove vegetables to a rack to cool. Wrap each fish cube
with 1/2 piece bacon. Place on platter seam side down.

To make kabob: Place a mushroom cap on one end
rounded side out. Next a zucchini slice, fish cube, pepper
slice, fish cube, shallot, whole potato, shallot, fish cube, red
pepper slice, fish cube, zucchini. Finish with mushroom cap
rounded side out.
mushroom cap • zucchini • fish • pepper • fish • shallot •
whole potato • shallot • fish • pepper • fish • zucchini •
mushroom cap

Place the 4 kabobs in a long baking pan. Top with 2 cups
herbed dressing. Cover with food wrap. Refrigerate for 1
hour or until needed.

To grill: Heat grill medium hot. Remove kabobs from pan.
Let excess dressing run off. Place kabobs on grill until
golden brown. Turn a quarter turn at a time until all sides
are golden brown. Check fish for doneness. Put on a platter.
Place broomed scallion on each end of skewer.

Chef John's Tips
- The bacon keeps the fish cubes moist.
- Chicken breasts can be boiled with the potatoes and
  shallots.

Grilled Fish Kabobs that Work Ingredients

- 16 fish cubes, 1" squares
- 1 cup seasoned flour (see recipe)
- 8 pieces bacon
- 1 quart water for boiling vegetables
- 1 tsp. salt
- 4 small red potatoes
- 8 shallots, peeled
- 1 Tbsp. olive oil
- 2 large red peppers, cut into 8 cubes
- 2 zucchini, cut in 8 -1/2" rounds
- 8 mushrooms, stems trimmed even to cap bottom
- 1/2 cup sherry
- 2 cups herbed dressing
- 4 long wooden or metal skewers
- 8 scallions

SERVES: 4 to 6

ROASTED FISH on a PLANK

Preheat oven to 400°.

Remove all fish scales, clean inside cavity well and remove gills and eyes.

Combine soft butter with white pepper, thyme, cornstarch and tarragon. Brush a thick layer of butter mixture inside cavity. With a potato peeler remove yellow skin from whole lemon in one piece. Place lemon zest inside cavity. Brush both sides of fish with butter mixture and roll in flour. Place on a sheet of aluminum foil in a large baking pan. Roast fish in a 400° oven until skin is golden brown and meat is milky white. Remove from oven and mist with fresh lemon juice. Serve on a hot large wooden plank.

Chef John's Tips

- Use cedar, oak or birch planks 1" thick, 10" wide and 24" long.

- Be sure the plank is clean and free of splinters before heating. On smooth side spray with oil to coat. Place in a 400° oven for 20 minutes. Place fish on the smooth side of the plank.

- Don't be alarmed if the plank may turn dark in color.

- Roasting time for a fish 4 to 6 lbs. is 25 minutes. Roasting time for a fish 6 to 8 lb. is 30 - 35 minutes.

Roasted Fish on a Plank
Ingredients

- 6 lbs. fish
- 1/2 cup whole butter, softened
- 1/8 tsp. white pepper
- 1 tsp. fresh thyme leaves, sliced fine
- 1 Tbsp. cornstarch
- 1 tsp. fresh tarragon, sliced fine
- 1 lemon for zest
- 2 cups seasoned flour (see recipe)

SERVES: 4 to 6

BAKED STUFFED FISH

Preheat oven to 350°.

Clean and scale fish. Remove gills, eyes and dorsal fin. Place fish on a piece of double thick aluminum foil. Salt and pepper cavity. Combine corn bread stuffing with tiny shrimp. Place inside fish cavity. Brush fish with butter. Place in the center of a large double-thick sheet of foil. Fold sides of foil over head and tail and roll into a tight cylinder. Place on a large shallow baking pan seam side down and bake in a 350° oven until internal temperature is 160°.

Use a meat thermometer to see if the fish is done.

Chef John's Tips

- A whole fish is a spectacular and ancient dish, naturally full of drama. This is your opportunity to show your creativity and inspire "oohs" and "ahs" from your guests.

- Remove bones from ribs through the inside cavity leaving the back bone intact to keep fish in one piece.

- A specific baking time cannot be given because each fish will cook differently.

Baked Stuffed Fish
Ingredients

- 1 whole fish, larger than 5 lbs.
- salt and pepper to taste
- 3 cups corn bread or fish and seafood
  stuffing (see Corn Bread stuffing recipe)
- 2 cups tiny shrimp
- 1/4 cup melted butter

SERVES: 4 to 6

FISH and ROASTED VEGETABLE NAPOLEONS

Wash all vegetables thoroughly. Slice eggplant and brush lightly with olive oil. Heat a large skillet. Add eggplant slices 4 at a time and sauté until golden brown on one side. Remove to a paper towel lined sheet pan placing brown side down. Brush sweet potato slices with olive oil and sauté golden brown on both sides. Remove to sheet pan. Repeat with zucchini slices and pineapple rings.

Slice tomatoes and season with salt, black pepper and thyme. Dredge fish in flour and sauté in 1 Tbsp. olive oil until golden brown on both sides. Remove to paper towel lined platter.

To build Napoleons, cover a baking sheet pan with aluminum foil. Brush with olive oil. Build all four Napoleons one at a time. First, place a slice of eggplant brown side up. Top with a slice of Cheddar cheese. Top with fish fillet. Sprinkle lemon pepper evenly over fish. Add zucchini slice, sweet potato, seasoned tomato slice, Mozzarella cheese, fish fillet, pineapple ring and second eggplant slice brown side down. Remove stem end and seeds from Anaheim pepper and stuff a sweet pickle inside pepper. Stick a sharp skewer through the stuffed Anaheim pepper and through the center of vegetable/fish stack. Place in a 350° oven for 25 minutes. Remove leaves from the bottom 3/4 of the rosemary sprigs and sharpen the ends. Remove from oven to warm plates. Replace skewers with rosemary sprigs. Serve with a lemon wedge.

Chef John's Tips

- This recipe is fun to prepare.
- If sweet potatoes are not available, use any large potato slices.

Fish and Roasted Vegetable Napoleons Ingredients

- 1 large eggplant, cut into 8 slices
- 1/4 cup olive oil
- 4 sweet potato round slices, 1/4" thick
- 4 zucchini slices, 1/4" thick and
  3" long
- 4 pineapple rings
- 4 jumbo sized tomato slices, 1/2" thick
- 1/4 tsp. salt
- 1/2 tsp. fresh ground black pepper
- 1 tsp. dry thyme
- 8 boneless fish fillets (2 to 3 oz. each)
- 1 Tbsp. flour
- 4 slices Cheddar cheese
- 1 tsp. lemon pepper
- 4 slices mozzarella cheese
- 4 Anaheim or large jalapeño peppers
- 4 large sweet pickles
- 4 sprigs rosemary
- 1 extra large lemon, cut in quarters

SERVES: 4

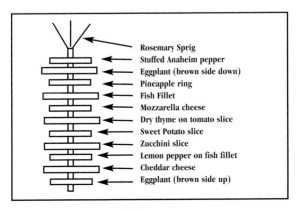

Rosemary Sprig
Stuffed Anaheim pepper
Eggplant (brown side down)
Pineapple ring
Fish Fillet
Mozzarella cheese
Dry thyme on tomato slice
Sweet Potato slice
Zucchini slice
Lemon pepper on fish fillet
Cheddar cheese
Eggplant (brown side up)

FISH PAPRIKOSH

Preheat oven to 350°.

Heat butter in a Dutch oven to a fast bubble. Add garlic, onions, red peppers and sauté until onions are tender. Combine flour, paprika, salt and white pepper. Add to onions and mix smooth with a wooden spoon. Add olives, mushrooms, wine, diced tomatoes and liquid, tomato purée and bring to a boil. Simmer for 15 minutes on low heat. Place fish on top of base. Cover and bake in a 350° oven for 20 minutes. Stir gently and serve. Top with sour cream and chopped parsley.

Chef John's Tips

- Be careful not to overcook fish as it will turn into a watery, crumbly mush. This is not a hint. It's an order!

- I make the base at home and bring it along to camp. Then simply reheat and add the fish in a covered Dutch oven over the camp fire.

Fish Paprikosh Ingredients

- 1/4 cup whole butter
- 2 cloves garlic, minced
- 2 cups onion, diced 1/2"
- 1 1/2 cups red pepper, cut in 1/2" cubes
- 1/4 cup flour
- 1 Tbsp. paprika
- 1 tsp. salt
- 1/4 tsp. white pepper
- 1/2 cup black olives, sliced 1/4"
- 1 cup mushrooms, sliced 1/2" thick
- 1 1/2 cups dry red wine
- 2 cups diced tomatoes and liquid
- 1 cup tomato purée
- 4 cups fish fillets, 2" pieces
- 1 cup sour cream and chopped parsley
  for garnish

SERVES: 4 to 6

HEARTLAND FISH HASH

In a large skillet heat oil until hot. Add onions, celery and red peppers. Sauté until onions are tender. Add potatoes, corn, pickles, thyme, salt and pepper. Toss to combine and cook on medium heat until the potatoes and corn are hot. Place fish pieces evenly over the base and cover. Cook on low heat for 3 minutes. Remove pan from heat and let sit, covered for 5 minutes. Remove cover and serve with poached or boiled eggs.

Chef John's Tips

- The reason to add fish last is not to over cook and break up the fish pieces when stirring.

Heartland Fish Hash
Ingredients

- 1/4 cup olive oil
- 1/2 cup red onions, diced 1/4" thick
- 1/2 cup celery, diced 1/4" thick
- 1 cup red peppers, diced 1/4" thick
- 2 cups red potatoes, boiled with skins on, diced 1/4" thick and cooled
- 1 cup frozen whole kernel corn
- 1/2 cup dill pickles, diced 1/4" thick
- 1 tsp. thyme, dry leaves
- 1 tsp. salt
- fresh black pepper to taste
- 2 cups fish fillets, diced 1" thick

SERVES: 4

DAY'S END CAMP FISH SALAD

In a large skillet, cook bacon brown and crisp. Remove with a slotted spoon and set aside. Add butter and onions and cook until tender. Dredge fillets in seasoned flour and place in skillet, skin side down. Cook light brown on both sides. Place fillets on top of cooked onions. Add potatoes, salt and pepper. Sauté until potatoes are hot. Split heads of Iceberg lettuce on 4 plates. Top with potatoes, onions, fish, cucumber, tomato cubes, bacon pieces, blue cheese and crushed crackers. Serve with 2 tablespoons French and 2 tablespoons Ranch dressing.

Chef John's Tips

- At the end of the day in camp, spending a short time to prepare and cook food in only one skillet is appealing to me.

- A soft tortilla on the bottom of the salad makes great eating and easy dish cleaning.

- This is a great dinner at home. I add avocados, cheese, sunflower seeds, cottage cheese, chopped dill pickles, hot cherry peppers and a cob of fresh sweet corn or two. For dessert I add a double scoop of ice cream and hot fudge on top of a chocolate cookie and milk to wash it down. For some reason, I always get nightmares after eating this!

Day's End Camp Fish Salad Ingredients

- 8 strips bacon, cut in quarters
- 1 Tbsp. butter
- 1 cup onions, sliced 1/4" thick
- 4 medium fish fillets, 6 to 8 oz. or 8 small fillets
- 1/2 cup seasoned flour (see recipe)
- 2 cups cooked potatoes, sliced 1/4" thick
- 1/2 tsp. salt
- 1/8 tsp. black pepper
- 2 heads Iceberg lettuce
- 1 peeled cucumber, cut into 1/4" cubes
- 2 tomatoes, cut into 1/2" cubes
- 1/2 cup blue cheese crumbles
- 8 to 10 crackers broken into pieces
- Red French salad dressing as needed
- Ranch salad dressing as needed

SERVES: 4

POPEYE FISH SANDWICH

Place fish steaks in a large ziplock bag with herb dressing. Refrigerate for 1 hour. Thoroughly wash and remove stems from fresh spinach.

To prepare onions, lay out a triple layer of paper towel. Place onion slices on paper towel and top with another triple thick layer of paper towels. With the palm of your hand, press on onion slices firmly to squeeze out juice. Turn onion slices over and repeat.

To cook fish, heat oil in a skillet. Remove fish from herb dressing and pan fry golden brown on both sides.

To assemble sandwich, slice hard rolls in half. Spread both sides of roll with honey mustard. On top half of each roll place 1 cup spinach, 1 slice cheese and onion slices. On bottom half place 1 piece fish and pineapple ring. Close sandwiches and serve.

Chef John's Tips

- This recipe also works well with all types of grilled saltwater fish steaks or cold leftover boneless fish.

- I sometimes toss in one or two of my favorite hot peppers!

Popeye Fish Sandwich Ingredients

- 4 - 6 to 8 oz. boneless fish steaks
- 1 cup herb dressing
- 4 cups fresh spinach leaves, stems removed
- 1 large red onion, peeled and cut in
  1/4" slices
- 2 Tbsp. vegetable oil
- 4 French or Italian hard rolls
- 1/3 cup honey mustard
- 4 - 1 oz. slices Dill Havarti cheese
- 4 slices pineapple rings

CRISPY COCONUT FISH

Sift chili powder, black pepper, garlic powder, mustard and seasoned flour into a pie plate. Combine fresh bread crumbs with shredded coconut. In an electric fry pan or deep fryer, heat oil to 375°. Dredge fish fillets in flour mixture. Shake off excess flour. Dip in egg wash. Shake off excess. Cover with coconut/bread crumb mixture. Deep fry until golden brown. Remove to a paper towel lined plate. Serve with flavored mayonnaise.

Chef John's Tips

- Fish fillets should not be thicker than 1/2" or longer than 3". Larger fillets will absorb too much oil.

- I enjoy combining 1 tablespoon of sugar and 1/2 teaspoon of cinnamon and sprinkle it lightly over the cooked fillets as soon as they are removed from the fryer. Then I splash each fillet with fresh lemon juice.

Crispy Coconut Fish
Ingredients

- 1 1/2 tsp. chili powder
- 1/4 tsp. black pepper
- 1/4 tsp. garlic powder
- 1/4 tsp. dry mustard
- 1 cup seasoned flour (see recipe)
- 1 cup fresh white bread crumbs
  (see recipe)
- 1 cup shredded coconut
- 2 cups vegetable oil
- 12 boneless pan fish fillets, with skins on
- 1 cup egg wash (see recipe)
- 1 cup Flavored Mayonnaise
  (see recipe)

SERVES: 4

PICKLED FISH

Fillet and skin fish making sure to remove all large bones. (Small bones will dissolve.) Cut into cubes. Put cubes in glass dish and cover with brine solution (step B) about 24 hours. Remove brine and rinse well with cold water. Put cubes back into dish and cover with white vinegar (step C). Cover dish and refrigerate for 48 hours. Drain and rinse in cold water. Put fish cubes in large glass jar. Make pickling solution (step D) by bringing pickling ingredients to a brisk boil for 3 minutes and cool to 160°. Then add to fish. Add the onions and red peppers (step E).

Cover and refrigerate for five days stirring or shaking jar once a day. Keep refrigerated and serve with crackers, cheese, sliced apples or rice cakes.

Chef John's Tips

- Northern pike, salmon or lake trout are perfect for this recipe. Saltwater fish can also be used.

- The pickling solution must be cooled to 160°. If the pickling solution is too hot, it will par cook the fish, making it mushy. If the pickling solution is too cold, it will not kill unwanted bacteria and the pickling flavor will not permeate the fish cubes.

Pickled Fish Ingredients

STEP A: Prepare Fish
8 cups raw fish fillets, cut into 1" cubes

STEP B: Make Brine Solution
1 cup pickling salt
6 cups water

STEP C:
Cover with 1 quart white wine vinegar

STEP D: Prepare Pickling Solution
1/2 cup brown sugar
2 cups white wine
3/4 cup white vinegar
2 Tbsp. pickling spice
2 small jalapeño pepper, seeds removed
2 tsp. juniper berries
2 tsp. fresh tarragon leaves

STEP E: Add Vegetables
1/2 cup diced onion
1/4 cup diced red peppers

SERVES: 10 - 12

NORTH COUNTRY PAELLA

This recipe takes a monstrous pan or skillet. A paella pan is wide and shallow with two handles. It is made with steel, cast iron or stainless steel lined copper. They can be found in specialty shops or call Chef John at the hotel/restaurant.

The most important part of this recipe is getting all the ingredients ready. This is a must before you start this paella dish.

In a Dutch oven, place wild rice, clam broth, white wine, butter, paprika, black pepper, garlic and whole shallots. Stir gently to combine. Cover and bake at 350° for 45 minutes. Remove from oven and hold for later.

While rice is baking, clean chicken pieces removing extra fat, skin and pin feathers. Remove the stem ends from peppers and tomatoes. Drain olives and artichoke hearts.

In a paella pan or large frying pan, heat olive oil until almost smoke hot. Roll chicken pieces in seasoned flour and shake off excess flour. Add to oil and brown well on both sides for about 15 minutes on medium heat being careful not to brown chicken. Push chicken to one side. Add sausages and brown on all sides. Add peppers, tomatoes and artichoke hearts. With a wooden spoon or spatula remove crust from bottom of the pan to keep food from sticking and burning. Cook vegetables for 3 minutes. Keep heat on medium.

(directions continued on next page)

Chef John's Tips

- This is a participation-cooking event. The more helpers, the better.

North Country Paella
Ingredients

- 2 lbs. wild rice
- 1 quart clam broth
- 2 cups dry white wine
- 1 lb. butter
- 1 Tbsp. dark paprika
- 1 Tbsp. coarsely ground black pepper
- 6 whole cloves garlic
- 12 shallots
- 6 chicken legs and thigh quarters
- 6 red peppers, stems removed
- 6 plum tomatoes, stems removed
- 1 cup large pimento stuffed olives
- 2 cups whole artichokes hearts
- 1 cup olive oil
- 1 cup seasoned flour (see recipe)
- 6 smoked venison sausages
- 1 1/2 lbs. sea legs (crab flavored fish)
- 6 - 8 to 10 oz. boneless fish fillets
  or steaks
- 2 bunches green onions, sliced in 1/4" rounds
- 6 tortilla shells

SERVES: 6

North Country Paella (continued)

Arrange chicken pieces, sausages and vegetables in order. Add cooked wild rice mixture evenly over top of base. Top rice with olives, sea leg pieces, fish fillets and green onions. Cover with tortilla shells to make it air tight. Reduce heat to low and simmer for 15 to 20 minutes. Remove tortilla shell and place on each dinner plate and let the fun begin. Have everyone serve themselves.

ONION JUMBOS with FISH ROLL-UPS

It makes no difference what color onions you use; only the size counts. Fill a large bowl half full of cold water and 1/3 cup cider vinegar. Gently plunge onions up and down to clean. Remove and set in a baking dish or Dutch oven stem end down. Cut 1/4" to 1/2" off the top. If onion will not set up straight, tell their mothers or cut a very thin slice off the bottom. Remove center with a melon ball scoop or teaspoon being careful to leave 1/4" thickness on sides and bottom.

Preheat oven to 375°.

Place flour and rub in a flat pan. Combine well. Coat each fish fillet. Do not shake off excess flour seasoning. Roll each fillet into a cylinder and place in the center of an onion. Top with soft butter. Place onion lid on top. Add chicken or fish stock and onion pieces from centers to dish. Cover and bake at 375° for 45 minutes. Remove cover and bake for 10 minutes letting outside of onions get crisp. Gently remove and serve with polenta, risotto, or spätzles.

Chef John's Tips

- Vinegar is added to the cleaning water because the acidity helps to kill bacteria.
- Popcorn shrimp, crab meat or scallop slices placed inside the fish rolls adds greatly to this dish.

Onion Jumbos with Fish Roll-ups Ingredients

- *4 of the largest onions you can find*
- *2 quarts water*
- *1/3 cup cider vinegar*
- *2 tsp. flour*
- *2 tsp. Chef John's Fish Rub (see recipe)*
- *4 - 4 to 6 oz. fillets, boneless*
- *2 Tbsp. whole butter, softened*
- *1 cup chicken or fish stock (see recipe)*

SERVES: 4

SCOUT CAMP FISH BAKE

Lay four large sheets of double-thick aluminum foil on a flat surface. Peel carrots and onions. Remove seeds from peppers and slice vegetables.

To build each fish bake. In the center of each foil sheet place a fish steak and top with 2 potato slices, 2 zucchini slices, 2 carrot slices, 1 onion slice, half red pepper. Sprinkle with thyme and lemon pepper. Top with a thick slice of butter and lemon juice.

Fold up foil to make a tight pouch. Place on medium heat side of camp fire or grill. Turn often to roast evenly. It takes about 30 minutes. (Or bake in a 375° oven for 1 hour.)

Chef John's Tips

- The thicker the fish steak or fillet the better. If using a tender fillet, place potatoes on bottom of stack first.

- Some of the simplest recipes are still the best. I was not a boy scout being a farm kid, but I made these fish bakes at 4-H camp.

Scout Camp Fish Bake
Ingredients

- 4 - 8 to 10 oz. fish steaks or slabs
- 2 large Idaho potatoes, sliced 1/2"
  thick, with skins on
- 4 zucchini, sliced 1/2" thick, 4" long
- 4 carrots, sliced 1/2" thick, 4" long
- 2 large onions, sliced 1/2" thick
- 2 red peppers, cut in half, seeded
  and stemmed
- 1 tsp. dry thyme
- 1 Tbsp. lemon pepper
- 1/2 lb. butter
- 1 Tbsp. fresh lemon juice

SERVES: 4

Fish Side Dishes

TARTAR SAUCE

- *3/4 cup dill pickles, diced 1/4"*
- *1/3 cup onion, diced 1/4"*
- *3/4 cup black olives, diced 1/4"*
- *1 cup mayonnaise*
- *1 cup sour cream*
- *1 Tbsp. sugar*
- *1 Tbsp. fresh lemon juice*
- *4 drops Tabasco sauce*
- *1 tsp. coarse ground black pepper*
- *2 tsp. Worcestershire sauce*

Dice crisp dill pickles, onions, black olives and place in a strainer and gently press mixture to remove excess liquid.

In a mixing bowl, place mayonnaise, sour cream, sugar, lemon juice, Tabasco, pepper and Worcestershire sauce and mix well. Add onions, pickles, black olives and gently fold in.

Remove from bowl and keep covered in refrigerator up to one week.

Chef John's Tips

- You can substitute green olives stuffed with pimentos for black olives.
- It is important to strain olives, pickles and onions well.

CHILI PEPPER TARTAR SAUCE

Tartar sauce recipe with the following additions:

- 2 jalapeño peppers, diced 1/4"

- 1 tsp. tarragon leaves

Remove seeds, white pulp and stem from jalapeño peppers. Dice into 1/4" pieces. Add peppers and tarragon leaves to tartar sauce. Mix and refrigerate

Chef John's Tips

- To turn up the heat, add hotter chili peppers or leave pepper seeds in the recipe.

GOURMET LEMONADE

Combine ingredients in a sauce pan and boil for 3 minutes. Remove from heat and let cool to room temperature. Store in refrigerator in a covered glass container until ready to use.

For 1 tall glass of lemonade, mix the following:

- 1/4 cup lemonade base
- 3 ice cubes
- 1 lemon cube
- 8 oz. cold water

To make lemon cubes:

Freeze fresh squeezed lemon juice in an ice cube tray. When frozen, remove to a double thick resealable bag. Add 1 lemon cube to each glass of lemonade. As the ice melts, it keeps the drink full of flavor.

Chef John's Tips

- The most important part of this recipe is to remove all white membrane from lemon zest with a potato peeler. The white membrane will make the lemon base bitter.

- For a pink color, add a little cranberry juice to lemon juice before freezing.

- To make the vanilla bean sugar, I put a vanilla bean split in half in a glass jar for one week with the sugar. Sometimes I like to add two vanilla beans.

Gourmet Lemonade Ingredients

- 1 cup fresh squeezed lemon juice

- zest of 2 lemons

- 2 cups sugar (vanilla bean sugar)

SERVES: 10

ONE-EYED JACKS

- 8 slices cinnamon bread, cut 1/2" thick
- 1 Tbsp. butter
- 8 large eggs

Batter: 3 eggs
*   1/2 cup Half and Half*
*   2 Tbsp. brown sugar*
*   1 tsp. vanilla*
*   1 tsp. cinnamon*

To Make Batter: Place all ingredients in a large bowl and whisk until smooth.

Cut center from bread slices with a 3" round cutter. Heat skillet to medium hot. Add 1/2 Tbsp. butter. Dip 4 slices bread one at a time in batter shaking off excess batter. Place in pan. Break one egg in the center of each piece and fry until egg coagulates and bread is golden brown. Turn and fry to desired doneness.

Serve 2 slices per person with syrup, jam and fried apples.

BAKING POWDER DUMPLINGS and VARIATIONS

- *2 eggs beaten*
- *1/4 cup milk*
- *1/2 tsp. salt*
- *2 Tbsp. oil or melted butter*
- *1 cup flour*
- *1 Tbsp. Cream of Wheat or Farina*
- *2 tsp. baking powder*

Beat eggs to a froth. Add milk, salt and oil.
Combine flour, Cream of Wheat and baking powder.
Add to liquid. Gently mix to combine.
Do not over mix.

Dip large spoon into boiling liquid. Dip spoon into batter and dip into boiling liquid. Continue until batter is gone. Cover and simmer 12 to 15minutes.

P. S. I love my dumplings with a ton of butter!

Variations:

> Add 2 tsp. fresh dill
> Add 2 tsp. fresh herbs
> Add 2 tsp. Parmesan cheese
> Add 2 tsp. diced shallots (cooked and cooled)
> Add 3 tsp. shredded cheese

SOUPY CAMPBELL BEANS

Drain kidney beans and butter beans. Place all ingredients into a heavy pot. Simmer uncovered on low heat for 45 minutes or until onions are tender stirring gently to keep from sticking.

Chef John's Tips

- I got this recipe in the submarine service from my leading cook, Soupy Campbell. These are great beans hot or cold!

- You can also add ground game. For my kids I brown 2 pounds ground venison, drain the fat and add to beans. My family calls this "Slumgovia".

Soupy Campbell Beans
Ingredients

- 1 can kidney beans (15 oz.)

- 1 can butter beans (15.5 oz.)

- 2 cans pork and beans (15 oz.)

- 1 cup brown sugar

- 1 1/4 cups onions, cut in small pieces

- 1/2 cup ketchup

- 2 tsp. yellow mustard

- 1/3 cup dill pickle juice

- 1/4 cup maple syrup

SERVES: 4

CUCUMBER SAUCE

- *8 oz. cottage cheese*
- *1 tsp. lemon juice*
- *1/2 tsp. lime juice*
- *1 pinch white pepper*
- *1/4 tsp. salt*
- *1/4 tsp. Worcestershire sauce*
- *1/2 cup mayonnaise*
- *1/4 tsp. tarragon leaves*
- *2/3 cup cucumbers, peeled and shredded*

MAKES 1 pint

In a blender container, place cottage cheese, lemon juice, lime juice, white pepper, salt, Worcestershire sauce, mayonnaise and tarragon. Blend smooth. Place in a bowl.

Peel and shred cucumbers. Add to cottage cheese purée and combine well. Chill and serve.

Chef John's Tips

- This is a very tasty sauce with all kinds of fish.
- To make this sauce on the lighter side, use low-fat mayonnaise and cottage cheese.

FRESH BREAD CRUMBS

- 1 pound loaf white bread

Remove crust from bottom of bread. Cut slices in half. Place in a food processor and make into medium to fine crumbs. A blender also works well. Add 4 half slices one at a time. Blend on medium speed to make crumbs. Remove crumbs to a bowl. Repeat until all crumbs are made.

For different flavors: use whole wheat bread, light rye bread or pumpernickel bread.

Chef John's Tips

- Making fresh bread crumbs is an important and often overlooked detail of cooking. Fresh bread crumbs are far superior to prepared crumbs which become overcooked, dry and tasteless.

- Only make as many crumbs as you need.

- Do not use leftover crumbs. You run the risk of food poisoning.

- If crumbs are refrigerated too long, they will mold.

CHEF JOHN'S FISH RUB

Combine all ingredients and keep in a tightly sealed container. Rub on fish fillets or fish steaks and place in a ziplock plastic bag with 2 Tbsp. vegetable oil for at least 2 hours to fuse the flavors. Grill or sauté.

Chef John's Tips

- The rub will not tenderize fish.
- There is no salt in this recipe as salt draws out the moisture from the fish. Salt should only be added after cooking.
- Please add any spices or herbs you like.

Chef John's Fish Rub Ingredients

- 1/2 tsp. garlic powder

- 1/2 tsp. freshly ground white pepper

- 1/2 tsp. dry thyme

- 1 Tbsp. dry tarragon

- 1/2 tsp. Hungarian paprika

- 1 tsp. onion powder

- 1/4 tsp. allspice

- 1/2 tsp. ground brown mustard seeds

- 1/2 tsp. dry dill weed

- 1 tsp. lemon crystals

SEASONED FLOUR

- 1 cup all-purpose flour
- 2 tsp. salt
- 1/8 tsp. white pepper

Combine well.

Chef John's Tips

- The reason for using white pepper is so that the flour does not appear to have black flecks.
- Never reuse excess flour.

CLARIFIED BUTTER

- 1 lb. butter

This is sometimes known as "drawn butter". Place butter in a sauce pan at low heat until it is completely melted. Remove all foam which rises to the top of liquid. Take from heat and let stand until all milk solids have fallen to the bottom of the pot. With a ladle, remove all clear oil and keep.

Makes: 1 1/2 cups (12 oz.)

Chef John's Tips

- I prefer to use half margarine and butter. The margarine will increase the smoke point temperature allowing the liquid to be heated to a higher temperature without burning.

CITRUS BUTTERS

LEMON BUTTER
- *1 lb. butter*
- *1/4 cup shallots, minced fine*
- *1 Tbsp. lemon juice*
- *4 drops hot pepper sauce*
- *1 pinch white pepper*
- *1/2 tsp. lemon zest, grated*
- *2 Tbsp. fresh chives, cut 1/4"*

In a small skillet heat 1 tablespoon butter to a fast bubble. Add shallots and sauté until tender. Add juice and simmer for 1 minute. Pour into a medium mixing bowl. Add hot pepper sauce, white pepper and zest. Add chives and remaining butter at room temperature. Mix well to combine.

Roll into a 1 inch diameter log and cover with a plastic food film. Chill or freeze. For service, cut a generous piece and top fish or serve with roll or biscuits.

VARIATIONS:

Lime Butter - add lime juice and zest
Orange Butter - add orange juice and zest
Tangerine Butter - add tangerine juice and zest
Grapefruit Butter - add grapefruit juice and zest

Chef John's Tips
- It is important to remove all white membrane from zest of citrus fruits as the membrane is very bitter.

GRANDMA SCHU'S HASH BROWNS

- 6 cups grated raw potatoes
- 2 tsp. fresh lemon juice
- 1/2 cup onions, diced 1/4"
- 1/2 cup heavy cream
- 1 tsp. salt
- 1/2 tsp. white pepper
- 1/4 cup butter

SERVES: 4

Grate or shred potatoes. Put potatoes and lemon juice in a bowl, and let sit for 10 minutes. Drain off excess liquids. Add onions, cream, salt and pepper and mix.

In a medium, non-stick frying pan, bring butter to a fast bubble. Add potato batter and cover. Cook on medium heat until potatoes are brown. Turn potatoes, cover, and steam through. Potatoes should be light brown on both sides. Remove from pan and cut into squares.

Chef John's Tips

- Be careful not to use too large a frying pan. Potato squares should be about two inches thick. If using an electric frying pan, cut potato cake in quarters before turning.

LONG GRAINED WHITE RICE

- *2 cups long grained white rice*
- *4 cups water*
- *1 tsp. salt*

SERVES: 4 to 6

Preheat oven to 350°.

Place rice in a deep bowl. Let cold water rise slowly over rice to fill bowl. Stir rice with a long handled spoon. All rice hulls and bad kernels will float to the top. Remove floaters. Pour water and rice into a strainer.

Place rice in a medium sized cake pan. Combine salt with cold water and pour over rice. Cover rice pan with foil and poke a dozen small holes into foil with a pencil. Place in a 350° oven for 1 hour. Water will be evaporated and rice will be tender and sticky when cooked. Remove foil. Fluff with a fork. For sticky rice, leave foil cover on when removed from oven.

Chef John's Tips

- Short and medium grained white rice are cooked the same way.

RICE PILAF and VARIATIONS

Preheat oven to 350°.

In a Dutch oven heat butter to a bubble. Add onions and sauté until tender. Add rice and stir with a wooden spoon for 30 seconds to coat well. Add stock and seasoning. Bring to a boil. Remove from heat. Cover with foil. Punch 8 to 10 pencil sized holes in foil. Bake at 350° for 45 minutes. When pilaf is done, bay leaf will be on top, the liquid evaporated and the rice tender.

Chef John's Tips

- For camping, this recipe can be made in advance and kept cool. Reheat as if making fried rice.

Rice Pilaf and Variations
Ingredients

- 1 1/2 Tbsp. butter
- 2 Tbsp. red onion, diced 1/4"thick
- 1 cup white long grained rice
- 2 cups chicken or fish stock (see fish stock recipe)
- 1/4 tsp. salt
- 1/8 tsp. black pepper, freshly ground
- 2 bay leaves

SERVES: 4

VARIATIONS WHEN ADDING STOCK:

Add 1/4 cup diced ham and 1/2 cup green peas (frozen or fresh)

Add 1/4 cup red peppers and 1/4 cup pine nuts

Add 1 cup small peeled raw shrimp

Add 1/2 cup pine nuts and 1 cup sliced fresh mushrooms

CORN BREAD STUFFING

Preheat oven to 350°. In a large skillet, heat butter to a fast bubble. Add onions, garlic, celery, peppers and sauté until onions are tender. Add pickles and sunflower seeds. Turn heat to low and simmer 10 minutes. Place in a large mixing bowl. Add corn bread and toss to combine. Do not over mix.

In a large bowl, place eggs, game or beef stock, spices, Worcestershire sauce, salt and pepper. Whisk to combine well. Add pears and corn bread mixture. Combine well. Place in a Dutch oven or covered baking dish. Bake stuffing in a 350° oven for about 1 hour.

VARIATIONS:

Maryland style: add 2 cups raw oysters and liquid as a last step. Very gently fold in the stuffing.

Southwestern style: add deseeded hot chili peppers cut in 1/4" cubes.

Heartland style: add 1 cup pork sausage with vegetables in first step.

Canadian style: add 1 1/2 cups smoked salmon pieces as the last step

Chef John's Tips

- Excess stuffing can be frozen in double thick resealable plastic bags.

- If you are not a fan of sunflower seeds, substitute walnut pieces

Corn Bread Stuffing Ingredients

- 1/2 cup salted butter
- 1 1/2 cups red onions, cut 1/4"
- 2 cloves garlic, minced fine
- 1 cup celery, cut in 1/4" slices
- 1 cup yellow or red pepper, cut in 1/4" cubes
- 1/2 cup sweet gherkin pickles, cut in 1/4" cubes
- 1/4 cup sunflower seeds
- 6 cups cubed corn bread, pieces cut in 1/2" cubes
- 3 eggs beaten
- 1 cup game or beef stock
- 2 tsp. thyme
- 1 tsp. tarragon
- 1 tsp. dry poultry seasoning
- 2 tsp. Worcestershire sauce
- 1/2 tsp. salt
- 1/2 tsp. freshly ground black pepper
- 1 cup fresh pears, peeled, cut in 1/2" cubes

SERVES: 1 1/2 quarts

JOHNNY CAKES and HUSH PUPPIES

Heat an electric griddle to 375°.

In a bowl, beat egg and yolks. Add salt and half the cornmeal. Stir to combine. Add baking powder and nutmeg to rest of the cornmeal. Add cornmeal mixture and vanilla to base. Add milk and stir until smooth. If batter is too thick, add milk one tablespoon at a time. Drop a tablespoon of batter on a 375° griddle. Fry until brown on both sides and serve with hot butter brown sugar or jam.

To make hush puppies, use the same recipe but add 1 cup diced onions and a little more cornmeal. Form into small cakes the size of a biscuit. Use a 1/4 cup measure scoop to form puppies. Fry puppies in 1" oil at 375°.

Drain on a paper towel and serve hot.

Chef John's Tips

- Johnny Cakes and Hush Puppies use the same recipe. Johnny Cakes are cooked on a griddle. Hush Puppies are fried in oil.

- To make hush puppies that bite, add diced chili peppers that bark.

Johnny Cakes and Hush Puppies Ingredients

- *1 egg*
- *2 egg yolks*
- *1/2 tsp. salt*
- *2 cups cornmeal*
- *1 tsp. baking powder*
- *1/4 tsp. nutmeg*
- *1 tsp. pure vanilla extract*
- *1 1/4 cups milk*

SERVES: 4

CHEF JOHN'S "Good Eatin" COBBLER

FRUIT BASE:

Combine all dry ingredients and sift. Place in a resealable plastic bag. Add raisins and close tight.

TO MAKE FRUIT FILLING:

In a Dutch oven, pour a 12-oz. can of soda. Bring to a brisk boil. Add fresh fruit and return to a boil. Add dry base and with a wooden spoon stir well to combine. Spoon biscuits over the top of the cobbler. Cover and bake in a 375° oven or over campfire coals for 30 minutes.

FOR DUTCH OVEN COOKING OVER A CAMPFIRE:

Place Dutch oven over white hot coals (about 3" to 4" above coals). If lid is concave, place 5 to 7 hot coals on the lid. Let bake for 30 minutes. Check for doneness.

Cobbler is done when biscuits are baked through. To test for doneness, when a little piece is broken off, the inside should be white and look like a sponge.

There are so many variables when checking for doneness. Start after about 20 minutes with variables. It could take less or more time depending on the altitude, outside temperature, thickness of Dutch oven and heat source of fire.

Chef John's "Good Eatin" Cobbler Ingredients

- 1 1/2 cups brown sugar
- 1 1/2 Tbsp. cornstarch
- 1 Tbsp. non-dairy creamer
- 1 Tbsp. non-fat dry milk
- 1/2 tsp. nutmeg
- 1/2 tsp cinnamon
- 2/3 cup raisins
- 1 - 12 oz. can soda (any flavor)
- 4 cups fresh fruit + liquid from fruit
- Biscuits (see recipe)

Chef John's Tips

- Canned fruit works well. Remember to drain off liquid and use it instead of canned soda

- It must be 12 oz. of liquid

- The biscuit dough is the same as for making biscuits alone. To make biscuits, simply brush Dutch oven with oil or butter. Form biscuits and bake at 400°s for 20 minutes covered.

- Kinds of fruit - all kinds of melons (with no seeds), apples, pears, peaches, strawberries, blueberries, raspberries, plums, pineapple, cherries. If you use rhubarb, add 3/4 cup extra sugar. This recipe can be made with peeled, seeded and diced winter squash or pumpkins. For this variation, add 1/2 teaspoon ground cloves.

SACHET BAG

- *1 Tbsp. chopped parsley, with stems*
- *1 tsp. thyme*
- *2 bay leaves*
- *1/2 tsp. black peppercorns*
- *3 crushed garlic cloves*
- *4 whole cloves*
- *Cheese cloth or tea ball*

Place all ingredients in a cheese cloth.

Chef John's Tips

- The purpose of a sachet bag is to produce a balance of seasoning for stocks and soups.
- The reason for the bag is to be able to remove all ingredients when desired. You could also use a large tea ball but the cheese cloth works better.

COCKTAIL SAUCE

- 1/2 cup horseradish, well-drained
- 1 cup tomato catsup
- 1 cup chili sauce
- 1/2 tsp. fresh cracked black pepper
- 1 Tbsp. lemon juice
- 3 drops Tabasco sauce
- 1 tsp. Worcestershire sauce
- 1/2 tsp. onion salt

Put horseradish in a strainer and let dry. Mix all ingredients thoroughly in a bowl. Place in a covered glass container and keep refrigerated.

HORSERADISH SAUCE

- 1/2 cup horseradish, well-drained
- 1/2 tsp. Worcestershire sauce
- 1 1/2 cups mayonnaise
- 3 Tbsp. sugar
- 4 drops Tabasco sauce

Place horseradish in a fine strainer and press out liquid until almost dry. Place all ingredients in a mixing bowl and mix well. Keep in a covered glass container and refrigerate.

ROUX

- *1 lb. margarine*
- *1 lb. flour*

In a heavy 2-quart sauce pot or baking dish, melt margarine, stir in flour and bake for 1 hour at 350°. Stir the mixture every 20 minutes. When cooked, the roux should be golden brown and the consistency of wheat sand.

It is always better to use roux at room temperature. Roux keeps well in the refrigerator or freezer.

Chef John's Tips

- Sauces and gravies are one of the most important components of great cooking. Roux thickens sauces and gravies. Although roux is only one of many cooking thickeners, I have concluded after 35 years of professional cooking that it is the best thickener.

- It is very important to weigh the flour for this recipe and not measure it.

- Pour roux into ice cube trays and freeze. When frozen, place in resealable plastic bags. Thaw 10 to 15 minutes before using.

FLAVORED MAYONNAISE

BASE
- *1 cup mayonnaise*
- *1/8 tsp. white pepper*
- *1/4 tsp. salt*
- *1/2 tsp. lemon juice*
- *1/2 tsp. Worcestershire sauce*
- *1 1/2 tsp. sugar*

In a bowl whisk all ingredients smooth. Place in a covered glass container in refrigerator until service.

For variations add one or a combination of the following ingredients to the base.

> 1 tsp. curry powder
>
> 1 tsp. Cajun spice mix
>
> 1 tsp. taco mix
>
> 1 Tbsp. fresh herbs, leaves chopped fine
>
> 1 tsp. lemon pepper (omit salt in base)
>
> 1 Tbsp. currant jelly
>
> 1 Tbsp. hot pepper jelly
>
> 1 roasted red pepper (seed and skin removed)
>
> 1 Tbsp. fresh blue cheese

Chef John's Tips

- Do not make too much mayonnaise at one time.
- If adding a seasoning with salt, leave out salt in base.

FISH STOCK

Fillet fish and store for future use. Save fish bones, skins with scales on and head. Remove eyes and gills and discard. Remove entrails and discard. Wash fish bones, skins and heads.

Peel carrots, clean onions, fennel, celery and mushrooms. Slice all vegetables 1/4" thick. In a stock pot heat oil. Add vegetables and cook on medium heat for 7 minutes. Add fish parts, sachet bag, white wine and ice cold water. Heat to a simmer. Water should just barely bubble. Skim off foam. Gently stir with a wooden spoon. Make sure nothing is stuck to the bottom of the pot. Simmer on low heat to reduce liquid volume by one half. Remove foam from the top with a ladle often. Strain liquid through a fine strainer. Strain a second time through a double cheese cloth or cotton dish towel.

Chef John's Tips

- If it were up to me, I would pass a law stating "Every fish head, all skin and bones must be used for stock."

- Fish bones are soft and if simmered at too high a heat or for too long, they will break down and make the stock bitter and cloudy.

Fish Stock Ingredients

- 5 lbs. fish bones, skin and heads
- 1 cup carrots, cut in 1/4" slices
- 2 cups whole white onions, cut in 1/4" slices
- 1 cup fresh fennel root, cut in 1/4" slices
- 2 cups celery, cut in 1/4" slices
- 1 cup mushroom caps, cut in 1/4" slices
- 2 tsp. vegetable oil
- 1 sachet bag (see recipe)
- 2 cups dry white wine
- 5 quarts cold water

MAKES 2 quarts

PIE CRUST

- *2 cups all-purpose flour*
- *1 tsp. salt*
- *1 1/4 cups shortening*
- *2/3 cup cold water*

In a large bowl, place flour and salt. Add shortening. Toss to make pieces the size of small marbles. Add ice cold water. Lightly toss enough to make a dough. Combine dough just enough to hold together. Use a pastry cloth or dusted board to roll out crust.

For pie shells, dot crust with a fork. Gently shake to shrink dough. Place in pie pan; place second pie pan on top. Trim excess dough from edges. Place pans in oven upside down and bake at 350° for 15 - 18 minutes. This keeps pies from blistering and bubbling.

This will make four single-crust or two double-crust 9" pies.

Chef John's Tips

- Bottom pie crust should weigh 8 ounces. Top crust should weigh 7 ounces for a 9" pan. Leftover pie crust dough freezes well. Cut into proper weight and freeze in individual bags. Too much flour will make the crust tough. Always remember to shake crust after putting in a pan. This will help shrink crust before baking.

CAMP FRIED APPLES

- *4 to 6 large apples*
- *1 cup brown sugar*
- *1/2 tsp. nutmeg*
- *1/2 tsp. cinnamon*
- *1/4 tsp. salt*
- *1/4 cup butter*
- *1 tsp. lemon juice*

Cut apples into quarters. Remove core, seeds and stem from each apple. Cut each quarter in 3 slices. Combine sugar, spices and salt. Heat a heavy pan over medium heat. Add butter and melt. Add apples and gently toss. Add sugar mix and cook until apples are just tender. Splash with lemon juice. Cover and let set for 3 minutes.

Chef John's Tips

- Serve this recipe with fish as a side dish.
- Top your pancakes with this recipe as a dessert.

ROASTED SWEET CORN

The most important step is to find ripe ears of sweet corn with no worms. Remove corn silk and place ears in a container with cold water for at least 30 minutes.

Just before removing ears from water, add vegetable oil to water. Remove one ear at a time. This will allow the oil to coat the husk. Roast ears over medium heat (about 375°). Roast on each side for 4 minutes. Turn ear 1/3 turn and repeat until all sides are roasted. Keep a close eye on the color of the kernels. When they become an orange yellow color, the ears are ready. Do not worry if the husk becomes dark brown or black.

To eat, peel husk back. Cover corn with butter. Sprinkle kernels with salt and black pepper.

Chef John's Tips

- If you have corn left over, simply cut kernels from cobs with a sharp knife and keep. Reheat in butter later.

- For extra flavor, brush cooked corn with barbecue sauce, garlic butter, powdered cheddar cheese or Cajun seasoning.

- If you are taking corn on a camping trip or picnic, place corn in a plastic resealable bag with ice. This will keep the corn cold and as the ice melts the husks absorb the moisture.

- Do nut put salt in the water for soaking as salt will make the corn tough.

- After covering corn with butter, you may want to roll corn in a warm tortilla shell.

Roasted Sweet Corn
Ingredients

- 8 ears sweet corn
- 2 quarts ice cold water
- 1/4 c. vegetable oil
- 1/2 lb. butter
- salt & pepper to taste

SERVES: 4

BISCUITS

- *2 1/2 cups biscuit mix*
- *1/2 cup dry potato flakes or pearls*
- *2 Tbsp. non-fat dry milk*
- *2 Tbsp. non-dairy creamer*
- *1/2 tsp. nutmeg*
- *1 tsp. baking powder*
- *1 cup very cold water*

In a one-gallon size plastic resealable bag, place all dry ingredients and seal tightly.

To make biscuits for cobbler:

Add 1 cup cold water to bag and knead mixture in the bag 30 times. Open bag. With a tablespoon, scoop out heaping spoons of dough. Place on top of cobbler filling. Make sure to leave room for biscuits to rise so they do not stick together. Cover pot and bake at 400° for 30 minutes.

Chef John's Tips

- It is a must to have a heavy cast iron Dutch oven.
- When baking over a campfire, do not put Dutch oven over open flames.

GRANDMA FLORENCE'S SWEDISH VEGETABLE CAKES

- 1 cup red onions, sliced julienne 1" thick
- 2 cups potatoes, skin on, sliced julienne 1" thick
- 1 cup carrots, peeled, sliced paper thin
- 2 cups fresh spinach, sliced julienne 1" thick
- 1/4 head iceberg lettuce, sliced julienne 1" thick
- 2 Tblsp. fresh cilantro leaves, sliced julienne 1" thick
- 1 Tbsp. Worcestershire sauce
- 1/4 cup heavy cream
- 2 eggs
- 1 1/2 cups flour
- 1 1/2 tsp. baking powder
- 1/2 tsp. black pepper
- 1/2 tsp. salt

Wash and cut vegetables into julienne pieces (1" x 1/8"). In a mixing bowl whisk Worcestershire sauce, heavy cream and eggs to a froth. In another bowl combine flour, baking powder, pepper and salt. Add vegetables to egg mixture and toss. Sprinkle flour mixture over top and gently fold in to combine well. Heat a large skillet with olive oil to about 400°. Drop mixture into skillet with a large spoon. Flatten to 1/2" thick cakes. Sauté on both sides to golden brown. Remove from pan and keep warm until served.

Chef John's Tips

- If you wish you can leave out the cream and use buttermilk.
- These are also great served for breakfast with eggs and fried fish.

EGG WASH

- *2 eggs*
- *1/4 cup milk*

Break eggs into a bowl. Add milk. Whisk to a froth.

Chef John's Tips

- Never keep egg wash after use as it is a medium for bacteria. If you need a small amount, make half a batch.

GAME GOURMET GALLERY

BOOKS

John Schumacher's New Prague Hotel Cookbook
Learn everything you need to know to prepare hundreds of Chef John's favorite dishes...including many popular items direct from the menu of the world famous New Prague Hotel!
Autographed Paper Back; 214 pages; illustrated: **$14.95**

Wild Game Cooking Made Easy
Wild Game Cooking Made Easy can make you a successful wild game cook by presenting gourmet quality recipes in an easy-to-use fashion.
Autographed hardcover; 191 pages; illustrated: **$19.95**

Fishing Cooking Made Easy
If you would like to prepare restaurant quality gourmet fish dishes, but don't have the time, training, staff or exotic ingredients of a professional chef, you will love this cookbook.
Autographed Hard Cover; 192 pages; illustrated; **$19.95**

Game Cookbook "For Good Eatin'" with Chef John Schumacher and Ron Schara • Fish Cookbook "For Good Eatin'" with Chef John Schumacher and Ron Schara
These twin books are for packing along when going to the cabin or camping.
Soft Cover; 80 pages; illustrated; **$12.95 each**

Professional Library Edition
Chef John's Cooking Made Easy Library, consisting of eight videos, three cookbooks and an original Chef John apron
Eight Videos; Three Autographed Cookbooks; Apron: **$114.95**

Getting Started Edition
Chef John's Cooking Made Easy Starter Library, consisting of two videos (*Fish and Game Cooking Made Easy and Game Feast*) and three cookbooks.
Two Videos; Three Autographed Cookbooks: **$59.95**

For Ordering Information:

phone: 1-800-283-2049

fax: 952-758-2400

also look for us at:

www.schumachershotel.com

VIDEOS

Fish and Game Cooking Made Easy
Watch and learn as Chef John & TV host Ron Schara lead you step by step through great ways of preparing wild game and fish.
Video; includes printed recipes. Price: **$12.95**

Fish Cooking Made Easy
Learn to create interesting and exceptionally tasty dishes with this amazingly versatile and often underestimated food.
Video. Price: **$12.95**

Delicious Morning Meals
In this video, Chef John shows you quick, simple and tasty ways to prepare fish for breakfast.
Video. Price: **$12.95**

A Taste of Wild Game: Camp Cooking
Join Chef John as he demonstrates his techniques of Camp cooking in a friendly, engaging and easy to follow manner.
Video. Price: **$12.95**

A Taste of Wild Game: Grilling
This video is the perfect companion for the outdoor chef. Learn the techniques of the Game Gourmet, Chef John Schumacher, as he teaches you the simple secrets to successful grilling.
Video. Price: **$12.95**

A Taste of Wild Game: Venison
The joy of the hunt can be significantly enhanced when you learn the secrets to preparing and cooking venison the Game Gourmet way!
Video. Price: **$12.95**

A Taste of Wild Game: Game Feast
On this video Chef John prepares three complete game feasts, including breakfast, lunch and dinner. Create your own "game feast" with the knowledge you gain from this video.
Video. Price: **$12.95**

A Taste of Wild Game: Jerky, Sausage and Slow Cooked Venison
Join Chef John in this informative video and learn how to make your own jerky and sausage.
Video. Price: **$12.95**

Big Game Field Care and Butchering
This twin pack of videos shows you how to field dress your animal and butcher your game at home. It also includes cutting roasts, steaks and proper grinding.
Price: **$14.95**

**Items in stock are usually shipped within 5 business days.
If paying by check or money order, please allow extra delivery time for them to clear. Sorry we cannot ship to P.O. Boxes, nor deliver C.O.D.**

**ALL ITEMS SHIPPED 4th CLASS.
Shipping + handling costs additional.
Minnesota residents add 6$\frac{1}{2}$% sales tax.**